Four in and New Orleans

BENJAMIN HOCHMAN
WITH CHRIS SCELFO

SP
SPORTS
PUBLISHING
L.L.C.

SportsPublishingLLC.com

ISBN 13: 978-1-59670-237-0

Front cover image by *Ft. Worth Star-Telegram*
Back cover image by AP Images

Publishers: Peter L. Bannon and Joseph J. Bannon Sr.
Senior managing editor: Susan M. Moyer
Acquisitions editor: Doug Hoepker
Developmental editor: Jennine Crucet
Art director: Dustin J. Hubbart
Interior design: Dustin J. Hubbart
Photo editor: Erin Linden-Levy

Sports Publishing L.L.C.
804 North Neil Street
Champaign, IL 61820
Phone: 1-877-424-2665
Fax: 217-363-2073
SportsPublishingLLC.com

Printed in the United States of America

Library of Congress Cataloging-in-Publication Data

Hochman, Benjamin, 1980-
  Fourth and New Orleans / Benjamin Hochman ; with Chris Scelfo.
    p. cm.
  Includes bibliographical references and index.
  ISBN 978-1-59670-237-0 (soft cover : alk. paper)
  1. Tulane University--Football. 2. Football--Louisiana--New Orleans. I.
Scelfo, Chris, 1963- II. Title.

GV958.T76H63 2007
796.332'630976335--dc22
                                        2007035802

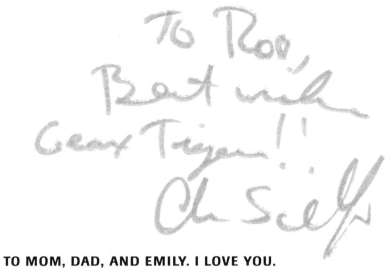

To Ron,
Best wishes
Geaux Tigers!!
Chris Scelfo

TO MOM, DAD, AND EMILY. I LOVE YOU.
−BENJAMIN HOCHMAN

TO NANCY, SARAH, AND JOSEPH−FOR BEING THERE FOR ME.
−CHRIS SCELFO

Contents

Foreword

by Deuce McAllister
of the New Orleans Saints

The inspiring story of the 2005 Tulane football team truly needs to be told.

I first met Coach Scelfo when I was in high school, when he was an assistant at Georgia, but our relationship really strengthened during my rookie year on the Saints. For me, Scelfo became more than a coach. He was a good one, to be sure, but he's also someone who cares about people. I've always admired the way he manages to be a father figure off the field, yet demands respect and the best from his players while on it. While keeping football a priority, Scelfo also manages to teach his team that their education is important, too. He wants what's best for his players as individuals, whether they are All-Americans or walk-ons.

During the storm and its aftermath, Scelfo had to deal with far more than was ever asked of any coach before him; he did everything from tracking down players' missing family members to getting them prepared for classes on a unfamiliar campus—all while preparing them to play football on Saturdays.

What happened to New Orleans sports teams after Hurricane Katrina was unprecedented. On the Saints, we had to pick up our teams and our families and move to a completely different city. Tulane had a similar fate. They were taken to the Jackson State University gym. Then they moved again and again, each time getting farther and farther from New Orleans while still worrying about their families back home. Being a man, especially one who plays the game of football, you always want to protect the people you love. It's hard to do that when you've been moved away and you don't have the assets because you're an amateur athlete. Because I play at the professional level, I had enough funds to buy a home in San Antonio and make sure my family was out of harm's way. But the Tulane players couldn't do that. Neither could most of the city of New Orleans.

During the 2005 season, Tulane was in an unfamiliar setting without family or friends. And they didn't have all their equipment; they'd only packed like they were leaving for a week. As a player on the Saints, I understood their frustration. After Hurricane Katrina, our team was displaced to San Antonio. NFL teams usually get the best of the best—facilities, catering, traveling. During our relocation period, there were times when we felt we were on the level of a high school team, just because of the facilities, living circumstances, and the preparation for games. We knew we weren't on an even playing field compared to the other NFL teams. We put it in perspective: at the end of the day, we're playing football, while other folks were jobless and homeless. But we wanted to represent New Orleans on the football field, and it was a struggle for us, as well as for Tulane, to do that.

That's why New Orleans teams truly banded together as brothers. The only thing Tulane players had was each other. Tulane competed and played hard, but that didn't show up in the win column. Tulane had a couple close games, where the emotions—and just being tired—caught up to them. They were a better team than their record showed. Still, ask those players in five or 10 years about their experience in Ruston, Louisiana, and they'll say it changed their lives for the better.

As for the Saints, we finished 3-13 in 2005, but you look at one or two games, and maybe the season would have turned around for us. You go back to the Falcons game in the Georgia Dome: we blocked a field goal, but there a penalty was called, and we were just deflated from that moment on. We'd been through the hurricane, had had to stay an extra week in Oakland, had moved to San Antonio, and had been living in a hotel for three weeks. There was so much that went wrong for us, we never really had anything go right on the field. We never caught that big break.

Especially after Katrina, you were really proud to say you were from New Orleans. Regardless of our record on the field, we were proud to say, "This is my city, this is my home, and I'm going to play as hard as I can for them." My heart really, truly went out to all the people in our city, just because you knew what they were going through, whether it was going to the Salvation Army for clothes or trying to find a job. By playing football, teams like the Saints and Tulane showed people in New Orleans that if we could bounce back, then maybe New Orleans as a whole could, too. And it showed the world that New Orleans was coming back.

Like the Saints, I think Tulane picked up fans they didn't even know they had, just because people could relate. I think everybody outside the region understands it now. Being from Mississippi, I understand how important football is to this region. Now, from Florida to Texas, California to New York, people understand how important football can be.

For the Saints to go from 3-13 one year to the NFC Championship Game the next season, I don't think you can put it into words. I think people can learn from Tulane's perseverance. The question is: will they learn? Hopefully, somebody's going to say, "I can survive, because look at these players. If you think life is tough on you, look at their situation."

It's unbelievable how much we take for granted. What are you going to do when you suddenly don't have anything? A lot of times, people wilt under that pressure. But Tulane persevered. Perseverance means being able to get up when all odds are against you, being able to rise after you've been knocked down over and over again, finding the strength in you to get back up. That's what Coach Scelfo and his team did during the 2005 season.

CHAPTER 1

For Others

Twenty minutes before kickoff, Tulane University's football players sat restlessly in an unfamiliar locker room. Some players cracked jokes to ease the tension; others plugged their ears with headphones and lost themselves in music. But there was nothing they could do to escape the weight of a hurricane-ravaged New Orleans resting on their shoulder pads.

These players were all hurricane evacuees that September of 2005. After scrambling to Jackson, Mississippi, as Hurricane Katrina bore down on the Gulf Coast, the team then relocated to Dallas, Texas, then to Ruston, Louisiana, and finally here—an antiquated locker room at Independence Stadium in Shreveport, Louisiana. This day—September 17, 2005—marked the first game of Tulane's historic season. The Green Wave, New Orleans' only college football team, would face Mississippi State in the first of 11 games in 11 stadiums in 11 cities, none of which would be their home field in New Orleans.

At his locker, senior Brandon Spincer solemnly bowed his head, praying quietly. A father of two, Spincer had spent sleepless nights after the storm worrying about the fate of his brother, who had chosen to ride out Katrina in New Orleans.

Across the locker room sat Bubba Terranova, whose mother's home was desecrated by Katrina. The receiver was in a daze, staring at his hands. Like so many of his teammates, Terranova's journey to Tulane's delayed season opener was wrought with life-altering questions, many of which had yet to be answered.

Tulane assistant coach Bill D'Ottavio strutted past the players, shattering the silence: "Cut it loose, let's have some fun out here," he belted. D'Ottavio sported a gray practice shirt and green mesh shorts, an outfit more appropriate for a weekday workout. It was hardly the look of a collegiate coach on game day. But like the rest of the coaching staff, his game-day attire was under water and still to be replaced. The team's game helmets had drowned, too, so the Green Wave wore practice helmets, green ones free of decals.

Assistant coach Greg Davis Jr. summoned the players together on the locker-room carpet, where each of them dropped to one knee. The door to the room swung open; head coach Chris Scelfo emerged.

In his thick Louisiana accent, Scelfo (pronounced "Sell-foe") hammered his words into the helmets of his players: "Defense, you've got to fly to the football. We have to create turnovers. Don't ask for them—I want you to create them. And you know how to create them—by peppering them, peppering them, peppering them! I want to stop the run. And secondary, do not go to sleep on your guy until the quarterback crosses the line!"

Anthony Cannon, the team's defensive star, locked eyes with his coach. The linebacker's apartment in New Orleans was flooded. The manifestations of his football memories—his letterman's jacket, his Hawaii Bowl ring—were likely ruined. To his right kneeled painfully homesick freshman Jordan Ellis. On this night, Ellis would see his parents for the first time since leaving for college. His hometown of Pass Christian, Mississippi, had been submerged in floodwater.

"Offense," Scelfo belted, "no penalties, no turnovers, stay ahead of the chains. All we've got to do is get first downs. Keep your composure, keep your poise!"

Starting quarterback Lester Ricard leaned against a locker, one of the few players standing. His head rose as Scelfo's inflection punched the words "composure" and "poise." The son of a preacher, Ricard had grown accustomed to such brash speech.

"Tulane's motto since the school started is: 'Not for thyself, but for others,'" the coach shouted. "'Not for thyself, but for others.' I don't want you thinking about nobody but the others in this room for the next three hours."

The coach's voice became round and fierce: "I want your *heart, mind, and soul* for three hours. You got it?"

Eighty-seven men responded in unison, "Yes sir!"

"I want your heart, mind, and soul! And I guaran-dang-tee you—the best team will win. Because the best team is in this locker room! And I'll be darned if we're going to feel sorry for ourselves, are we?"

"No sir!"

"ARE WE?"

"NO SIR!"

"We're going to go out there and do what?"

"WIN!"

And with that, 87 players erupted from their stances and charged through the tunnel at Independence Stadium, their united roar reverberating through the stadium's belly.

o   o   o

Even shirtless men sweat in the August heat in New Orleans. But despite high temperatures, the month of August is the time for football teams to shake off rust and sharpen their skills. It's during this month that players become bonded by teamwork and branded with desire. August of 2005 started that way for Tulane. Dozens of players—linebackers with perfect physiques, linemen with bellies that had succumbed to gravity—ran wind sprints on Tulane's practice field. It was the ritual that followed every Tulane preseason practice. At times, the last group running would be those hefty linemen, whose mouths wheezed like steamboat whistles. And so, the svelte senior linebackers would run extra sprints with the big boys, pushing their teammates to run through the heat, not from it.

It was such determination that was going to give Tulane the edge against Southern Miss, their first opponent on the 2005 schedule. The previous season, Tulane was a missed field goal away from bowl eligibility. And heading into 2005, most of the Green Wave's marquee players were back, including the starting quarterback, running back, and three veteran offensive linemen. On defense, only three starters had graduated. That left Tulane with an experienced roster primed for a big year. And with Conference USA's realignment—the conference lost football powerhouse Louisville and several other schools, replaced by weaker competition—the Green Wave's schedule was considered to be more easygoing than in previous seasons. Perfection, the team believed, was possible.

Since Coach Scelfo's first full season in 1999, Tulane was perennially on the verge of greatness, armed with a string of statistically gluttonous NFL-bound quarterbacks, but plagued with a conference lead in "what ifs." In 2000, a bowl-eligible team was denied a bid. Three years later, a star-studded cast suffered innumerable injuries, at one point fielding more healthy kickers than defensive ends. Even when the team did get invited to a bowl game in 2002, it was asked to travel to the Hawaii Bowl, where it would face the University of Hawaii Warriors on their home field. They won the game, however, thanks to a 30-point second-half comeback. Many of the freshmen on that 2002 team were the senior leaders heading into 2005.

The 2004 season, which saw Tulane post a 5-6 record but win four of its final six games, was to be a harbinger of good things to come. The 2005 team gelled in training camp, which only further served to raise expectations: Tulane was headed for a bowl game.

That August, the team lived together in Butler Hall, an honors dorm during the fall and spring but a football fraternity house in the summer. After sweating together during the day, the players would bond together at night, with as many as 15 football players squeezing into a tiny room to watch the HBO miniseries *Band of Brothers,* which chronicled a group of young men who formed one of the Army's first paratroopers squadrons in World War II. Others would play video games; guys who competed for starting roster spots during the day vied for *Halo* supremacy at night. Punter Chris Beckman, a country boy, would strum his guitar and sing country songs, while lineman

Frank Morton, a city boy, would answer his teammate's twang by rapping and dancing.

The bonding didn't happen overnight, but without fail—and often with force—it did happen. One night, the older players humbled the youngsters in a rite of passage, an act of initiation into the Green Wave family. The entrance fee: a shaved head. No one was above paying dues. Ricard, the strapping incumbent of the NFL-launching quarterback job, took the liberty of shaving the head of freshman Anthony Scelfo, the nephew of the head coach and son of offensive coordinator Frank Scelfo. Ricard saw it as only fair: with all the pain Frank Scelfo was putting *him* through on the field, it was only right for Anthony to share in the misery.

On August 20, 2005, nine days before Hurricane Katrina, the players relaxed in Butler Hall, passing around that day's copy of New Orleans' daily newspaper, The *Times-Picayune*. John DeShazier's sports column caught their attention with its headline: "Tulane poised for more success."

The column began: "Shhhh, quiet. Listen. No, really. Listen. Hear that sound—or, perhaps more accurately, the lack of it? It's calm, and, for the first time in a long time, it's surrounding Tulane's football team at the opening of a season. No waves are battering the Wave, not right now, anyway . . ."

CHAPTER 2

Evacuation

*F*or months, Chris Scelfo had methodically prepared his team for success as their 2005 season opener loomed in the distance. It wasn't uncommon for the janitor at the school's training facilities to beat Scelfo home at night; the coach spent many late evenings in his office, studying film and revising the playbook. The team's early-morning weight-lifting sessions were followed by meetings followed by more meetings followed by practice, then followed by meetings to discuss the practice.

On Sunday, August 28, 2005, everything that Scelfo and his team had worked so diligently to create was shaken like an Etch-A-Sketch and erased. He looked at his boys—so youthful, so naïve—and ordered them to pack a bag and then call their parents. A pair of tour busses sat parked outside Tulane's Wilson Center, the athletic department's hub, prepared to drive the Tulane football team out of New Orleans. Hurricane Katrina was on its way.

The busses were originally supposed to take the team to the Louisiana Superdome for practice. Although the athletic department had arranged for out-of-town busses to evacuate the team, Scelfo knew that the traffic and chaos caused by the citywide evacuation orders would prevent that transportation from arriving in New Orleans. So instead, he held the practice busses, the team's only means of escape. Those practice busses would eventually escort the team to safety at Jackson State University in Jackson, Mississippi, 190 miles north of New Orleans.

Players boarded the busses with their backpacks while Scelfo's staff loaded practice gear—shoulder pads, helmets, cleats, and whistles—into the busses' storage bays. Their first game of the season, against Southern Miss, was scheduled for the next weekend, so the staff packed the team's road uniforms just in case. Most players had only the clothes on their backs.

That morning, with his family already evacuated to Arkansas and meteorologists screaming at him through his television, Scelfo had known he had to get his team out of New Orleans, and soon. The Tulane women's soccer team was also at the Wilson Center in need of safe transport, so they joined the fray. As the teams finished boarding, a group of international students, new to campus, wandered over. They were to begin classes on Wednesday, and had no clue what to do. Scelfo made room for them on his bus. At 10:30 that morning, the football team, the soccer team, and the handful of international students fled campus on the two charters. Scelfo and his football staff followed in vans.

At the corner of Ben Weiner Drive and Claiborne Avenue, a taxi pulled alongside Scelfo's van and unloaded a mother, a father, two daughters, and several suitcases. Scelfo rolled down his window, finding the scene a bit odd, and asked if he could help the new arrivals.

"We just flew in from Canada. My daughter's on the swim team," the father replied. "We're not sure what to do."

But Scelfo knew: he made room for the new passengers, and once everyone was safely on board, the Tulane convoy rumbled on through the eerily empty streets of Orleans Parish, onto Interstate 10 West, and finally onto Interstate 55 North.

The coaching staff cut the tension with some humor. Nestled into one van with the coaches was a young student from Saudi Arabia who had arrived on campus that day. The coaches found out that he had a soccer background and joked that their special teams woes were over—they had found their kicker.

On the bus, a few players pressed their cheeks to the windows, noting the calm of the city. Rumors, hurricane "what ifs," were beginning to run up and down the bus aisles. Locals like Spincer reassured teammates that hurricanes don't hit New Orleans. But Spincer also knew that *if* an unlikely hurricane did hit New Orleans, the port city would be reduced to a port. Linebacker coach and New Orleans native Garret Chachere was wary of the storm and its impact on the team, but even more so of the damage it could do to the city he loved. Like most people who were groomed in the city, Chachere was raised with a fierce pride—and an accent, too.

Natives of the Big Easy were bred with a high metabolism and an even higher alcohol tolerance. New Orleans is a lifestyle, and those who call it home consider it an honor to reside in such a city. "Like New Orleans' famous dish, it is a gumbo here," said Chachere, who played ball at Tulane, married a woman named Duplessis, and adores the Southern cuisine at Dunbar's Creole Cooking, a restaurant well known by locals. "New Orleans is a mixture of people. It's a mixture of cultures, and that is what makes New Orleans different. You know, a lot of cities have this and that, but there's a culture here, and there is a bonding that you really cannot get anywhere else. And this may be good and bad—well, it is good and bad to New Orleans—but there are a lot of people here that have never been anywhere else. So they don't know anything else. They want to know New Orleans—that's it."

Such stubborn pride and acclaimed diversity is obvious throughout the city. In the French Quarter, where architecture has been preserved from centuries past, you can stumble upon a world-renowned restaurant, a pristine art gallery, a multi-leveled dance club, and an enigmatic hole-in-the-wall bar all before you finish your cocktail-to-go. New Orleans is where "Jazz funerals" are about mourning, but also celebrating. It's where a plaque in the back of the Maple Leaf bar reads: "Everette Maddox / Poet / 1944-1989 / 'He was a mess.'"

Tulane—or "TOO-lane" as some locals say it—is the largest employer in New Orleans, an emblematic mainstay of the city it calls home. While Tulane's student population arrives from Slidell to Saudi Arabia, everyone becomes infected by "Nawlins" soon enough. As he rushed out of town without a proper goodbye, Chachere felt a tug at his heartstrings, and restlessness in his gut.

It took the convoy six hours to travel the 60 miles to Hammond, Louisiana, and another five hours to make it to Jackson, Mississippi. At roughly 9:30 p.m., the beleaguered Green Wave arrived at the doorstep of the T.B. Ellis Gymnasium on the campus of Jackson State. Coach Scelfo had made phone calls to other Tulane officials, desperate to organize some semblance of comfort for his team; yet there was nothing to sleep on save for a small stack of mattresses. After the daylong odyssey, the majority of players would have to sleep on a hardwood gym floor. A furious Scelfo drove to Wal-Mart to purchase some essential supplies for his team, and later caught a bit of shuteye in the hallway of the gym with his assistants.

Late that Sunday night, Scelfo found a quiet area and called his wife, Nancy, on his cell phone—one of the last calls he would be able to make before cell towers throughout the region gave in to the storm. Nancy was safe, asleep in Arkansas. Scelfo told his wife that they were in Jackson.

Between yawns, Nancy said, "Chris, I think it's going to be bad."

CHAPTER 3

Touchdown

*O*n the morning of Monday, August 29, 2005, the Tulane football team awoke to the sounds of harsh winds and bullet-like raindrops punishing the roof of the gymnasium. A group of players huddled around an open gym door, in awe of the weather outside. Across the street stood the wooden frame of a church under construction; within seconds, it would collapse to the ground. "With the wind that strong, I just imagined what was going on in New Orleans," said Sean Lucas, a senior safety.

Two days prior, a peppy Tulane football team had practiced at the Superdome, a rather humdrum happening for any sports venue, much less this Mecca for memorable sporting events. At the Superdome, Muhammad Ali lost his title; Roberto Duran uttered "No Mas;" Pistol Pete dazzled; North Carolina freshman Michael Jordan hit a championship-winning jumper; Michigan's Chris Webber called The Timeout; Da' Bears shuffled to a Super

Bowl title; Carmelo Anthony became Carmelo Anthony; Tom Brady became Tom Brady; the Louisiana State University Tigers captured the 2003 NCAA football championship. Tulane, meanwhile, had just held a practice, as usual. That Monday morning, they had no idea of their accomplishment: They were the last sports team inside the Superdome, before the Superdome became *The Superdome*—the ravaged image of a beleaguered city.

Those who say "ignorance is bliss" have never encountered the sort of startled displacement that a hurricane like Katrina can induce. Inside the Jackson State gym on Monday afternoon, members of the Tulane football team crowded together, completely unaware of the extent of damage in New Orleans. They knew only of their immediate surroundings and what little information they had been able to gather through poor cell phone reception and word of mouth.

Brandon Spincer was a frightened kid inside the body of a chiseled, cocksure senior linebacker. He eulogized his city in his soft voice, telling his teammates about his time growing up in the streets of New Orleans. Spincer knew his two children—six-year-old Branisha and one-year-old Brandon Jr.—were safe with their mother. But that solace couldn't put his children in his arms at that moment, and so he talked, out of fear for the worst, of his hometown.

Freshman Jordan Ellis, a native of coastal Pass Christian, Mississippi, knew his family was safe from harm, because they had evacuated to Jackson, too. But Ellis was told he couldn't leave the gym to visit them, so he sat on the gym floor while fright gnawed at his stomach. He had spent the entire day pounding his thumb on his cell phone keys, hoping a number would somehow dial. But just as the infuriating rain continued to assault the roof above his head, his phone refused to get a signal.

His teammate, receiver Bubba Terranova, shared his frustration. Terranova had not gone so long as a day without talking to his mom, Patti, since he had been given his cell phone. Not that he was an effusive chatterbox who abused daytime minutes, but Bubba liked to hear his mother's calming voice. For a guy who outwardly looked as emotional as a statue, hearing his mother call him "baby" sent a gentle tingle up his spine. Now his mother was like him, on the run from Katrina after abandoning the family home in Slidell, Louisiana, a small city resting just north of New Orleans, across Lake Pontchartrain. He wondered about his mother's safety, but could find no answers. Like everyone else stuck in that gymnasium, he was stuck listening to the same rumors: bodies from a graveyard were floating down the streets of New Orleans; water levels had reached the fourth floor of the student dorms; the entire city was now part of the Gulf of Mexico. Nobody knew anything for certain.

Then the power went out, leaving the team completely cut off from the outside world in a dark, foreign gym. Many of the women on the soccer team, who had shared the evacuation buses with the football team, began to cry. Dinner was served: small, cold sandwiches that hardly satisfied the 250-pound men. The team wrestled with their blankets and comforters as the darkness of day spilled into the darkness of night, preparing for a second night of sleep on a hard gym floor.

Coach Scelfo decided to take action, to do something—*any-thing*—to try to take his players' minds off the storm. With any luck, it would do the trick for him, too. He gathered his team's seniors and asked them to coordinate a workout, something to get the team sweating.

In boxer shorts and bare feet, the Tulane football team did sit-ups, push-ups, and ran up and down the gym's bleachers, chanting in unison, "Beat Southern Miss! Beat Southern Miss!" The mood shifted. No longer was the team thinking of its woes; at that moment, it was focused on its next opponent, on football, on a task at hand, on being a team.

But the feeling couldn't last; when the activity ended, so too did the comfort of a retreat from reality. Eric Schumann, Tulane's defensive coordinator, began to doze off on a bench. His son, Glenn, was there, too, and spotted his dad's head bobbing while sitting up. "Dad, you look like a homeless person," his son said. Glenn then paused and continued, "We are homeless!" That story, first recounted to ESPN writer Ivan Maisel, became the poignant encapsulation of Tulane football. Like so many from New Orleans, the team was displaced, a feeling they would have to learn to tolerate in the coming months. But what they could not tolerate, above all else, was the uncertainty of the situation—the not knowing, and the fear that comes with the territory.

That night, Coach Scelfo's attention was directed toward two vital missions: one, locating the family of every player on his team, so that doubts could be dismissed; and two, getting the hell out of Jackson. The longer he sat in that gym, the angrier he became. He decided to make a plea for his players' sake. He could see the wear and tear on their faces, and it ate at him. On Tuesday morning, he approached Tulane Athletic Director Rick Dickson and gave him a simple directive: "We've got to get out of here," Coach Scelfo told him. "I don't care where we go or how we get there. This is inhumane. There's no air conditioning. These kids are locked up in here. We don't know what's going on in New Orleans."

What was going on in New Orleans was utter chaos, the likes of which the city had never seen. In neighboring Lake Pontchartrain, boats were piled up on each other like a stack of flapjacks.

Nearly 30,000 citizens pushed their way into the Superdome trying to find shelter. At the Morial Convention Center, 15,000 hungry hurricane victims convened. Despite the rumors of murder, death, and violence, these people were the lucky ones, safe from floodwaters and devastating winds. Thousands of others were left stranded in the attics of their homes with no evacuation route at hand, unaware that on Tuesday the levees would break and eighty percent of New Orleans would be under water.

Scelfo was able to organize busses to transport the team from Jackson to Dallas, thanks to some help from player Sean Carney's father, who owned a bus company. Conference USA administration had arranged for the team to stay at the Dallas Doubletree Hotel once they reached the city.

On Interstate 20, the team's busses grumbled to a halt at a truck stop outside of Shreveport, Louisiana. Inside the truck stop, a player spotted a tiny television. Soon, a crowd of players gathered, each dumbstruck by what they saw on the screen.

"On the screen was CNN," safety Sean Lucas recalled, "and we saw people with TVs, looting, running through water. I'm thinking that it's a third world country somewhere. I had no idea it was New Orleans. I thought there was a war or something going on. When they flashed the words 'New Orleans' on the screen, it just kind of hit me—man, I just left that place. What happened?"

That weekend began at the Superdome, where 6-foot-5, senior quarterback Lester Ricard had lofted touchdown passes to a brigade of wide receivers. Now, nearly three and a half days later, the players were headed to a second random city while stranded families slept on the Superdome turf holding each other because, in many cases, that was all they had.

Boarding the bus to depart, Ricard was no longer the strapping quarterback; he had watched those images on the television and instantly morphed into the preacher's son. He held his head in his hands, crying incessantly, unable to relinquish one haunting image from the broadcast of a shaken man recounting his ultimate loss.

"They were talking about a guy on top of his roof," Ricard remembered. "His wife was in his right hand, and his three babies were in his other. And his wife was slipping. The current from the water was pulling her. And she said, 'Just let me go, and make sure my babies are safe.'"

The rumors were no more. The players had run smack into reality, stunned by the notion that things were even worse than they had imagined.

The busses arrived at the Dallas Doubletree Hotel at 4 a.m. on Wednesday, August 31.

Coach Scelfo hadn't slept since New Orleans. He slid under the clean sheets but could do nothing besides toss and turn.

One of his two objectives had been met: his team had left the gym floor for the more relaxed setting of a hotel. But his second objective—to comfort his players by establishing communication with their families—was far from completed. His own family was in another state. His campus was flooded. His season was in flux. His team was scared.

He realized at that moment that he could not worry about next week, next month, or the next game on the schedule; he had to worry only about tomorrow.

CHAPTER 4

Roots

S am Scelfo shared the same birthday, September 30, as his son, Chris. Their birthday typically fell on the same weekend as the Sugar Cane Festival, a celebration held at the beginning of harvest season in their hometown of New Iberia, Louisiana, just a short drive from the Gulf of Mexico. Dad would host a barbecue and his eight kids, scattered across the state, would come home, stain their T-shirts with barbecue sauce, and listen to stories about dad's coaching days, when men were tougher and the workdays longer.

On October 1, 1982, Chris Scelfo hugged his father goodbye after a relaxing birthday weekend and drove back north to Monroe, Louisiana, where he was in his second year of college at Northeast Louisiana. Four days later, he prepared to drive back to New Iberia for his father's funeral. Sam Scelfo had suffered a fatal heart attack at the age of 63.

Sitting silent in his dorm room, Chris, then just a shocked 19-year-old, searched his soul for answers. How could his dad, always the strong, able support for a large family, no longer be there?

On the five-hour drive home from Monroe, Chris reminisced about his father. By himself, he could hide from reality, veiled in memories. But once Interstate 49 spilled onto the dusty roads of New Iberia, Chris' stomach began to knot. *I've never been to a funeral before,* he realized. More unfamiliarity awaited him at home.

In preparation for the service, Chris pulled on a stiff, neglected sport coat—one of his father's—and braced himself for his first outing without dad. The Scelfos were not a fashionable family, nor did they have a recurring need or desire to dress up. Sam Scelfos' fashion sense entailed polyester pants, golf shirts, and rubber-soled shoes; on the day of his funeral, he wore a plain gray suit in his open casket.

Before the entire town filled the church pews like they filled the stadium for a Friday night football game, the Scelfos sat in the first rows of a lonely church awaiting the start of the funeral service. Sydney Scelfo, Sam's sweetheart-turned-soul mate, grieved in sudden shrieks. The older siblings squeezed the younger siblings. Chris, helpless, stared at his dad's casket. *There lies my rock,* he thought. Chris would later call that service the hardest 30 minutes of his life.

○ ○ ○

The only thing small-town New Iberia has in common with the country of Italy is that their names both contain vowels. But that didn't stop Salvatore Sam Scelfo from immigrating to central Louisiana in 1926. As if conditioning himself for a new life, he decided to go by Sam Paul Scelfo. It wouldn't be until his death that his family would discover his given name on his birth certificate. The displaced Italian became an adopted "Luuusanian," raised among Cajuns with names like Boudreaux and appetites for étouffée. He married a Cajun-French girl and they built a home in Abbeville, Louisiana, and later one in near-by New Iberia, where there were as many movie theatres as mayors, where collars only came in blue.

The Scelfos house in New Iberia was a quaint four-bed-room, two-story, cinder-block home, comfortable for five but shelter for 10. There was only one air-conditioning unit, and that was upstairs where the daughters slept. All five of the sons slept like sardines on mattresses in the downstairs heat. By day they would fight over who got to be Archie Manning in front-yard football; by night they would fight over who would sleep closest to the lone fan.

Chris Scelfo was 10 years old when he first fell in love. Every night at the dinner table he would listen as his older brothers revealed the stories behind their scrapes and scars. That year, he would earn his own chance to tell such stories after joining a youth football team. The day he received his uni-form, he wore it to bed. He played baseball, too, but that was just a diversion to fill time until football season began. Football was fascinating, exhilarating. Football was what dad coached and his brothers played. Football made a boy a man, and a man a Scelfo.

The boys all learned the sport from a former Marine with a rotund stomach and a robust voice—their father. Sam Scelfo wasn't "old school;" he *was* the old school. He coached players with his snarl, not his heart, showing affection for his team by screaming louder and louder. "Good enough" was not a phrase in his vocabulary.

Chris recalls his dad's inability to accept satisfaction. To the old man, Chris could always do better. Deep down Sam might have been content, but he would never admit that to his son.

Sam coached high school football in small-town Louisiana, where the football coach is the pillar of the community—unless, of course, he's on a losing streak. He coached in towns like Abbeville and Crowley for three decades, dismissing a quartet of heart attacks as inconveniences on his path to victories. He held his players to high standards and was no less hard on himself. In 1958, five years before Chris was born, Sam was the head coach in Abbeville. Thirty kids showed up on a sweltering August afternoon for their first football practice and soon found themselves in boot camp. Only 13 of those players refused to quit. Several weeks later, those 13 kids won the Louisiana state championship.

"His big thing was, 'You gonna do things right, and you gonna do them hard,'" Chris recalls. "And that is the same way he was with us children. If we chose to start something, we had to finish it. He took that Abbeville team and said, 'Hey, this is what we have. Now we gonna make the best of it, and whatever obstacles are put in front of us, we gonna finish it.'"

Chris still cherishes a blurry old photograph of that team.

○ ○ ○

Sam Scelfo wouldn't buy a new car just to have a new car; he would only buy a new car because his previous car was, despite his attempts, beyond repair. He made due with what he had at hand, a lesson he impressed upon his boys when they

22

whined about sporting equipment that had been worn down from overuse. "Dad had more ways to tie up a baseball glove and make it work," Chris Scelfo recalls with a laugh.

Sam raised his children using a strict sense of right and wrong, imploring them to earn their desires and respect their elders. Dad laid down the law: Adults were to be addressed as "sir" or "ma'am," and curfew was midnight, even on prom night.

Much as he refrained from showing affection toward his team, Sam did the same with his kids, who were more likely to get a scolding from daddy rather than a hug. Chris explained his father's mentality when it came to showing affection: "Once you hug one, then you gotta hug the other seven, and soon the day was done." By ruling with an iron fist, Sam stayed involved in his kids' lives. He was there for advice, and was not shy about doling it out if the report cards featured letters too far into the alphabet. He approved his children's friendships, weeding out undesirable company as necessary.

While dad made the rules, mom managed the household. Sydney Scelfo was a virtuous woman, a math teacher with an angelic persona, known for her striking, black curly hair. Sam may have been the guts of the family, but Sydney was the soul. She watched more sporting events than a bookie, bouncing from ballpark to gymnasium, watching son after son in addition to Sam. Chris remembers an awards banquet he was to appear at during his freshman year at New Iberia High. A torrential downpour had flooded the roads, but Sydney was not going to miss the event, even if it meant fording the road to get there. When her son received his football plaque, she clapped the loudest. She was the perfect foil to her husband. Eternally maternal and ever-present in the kitchen, Sydney was a doting and loyal mother and wife, as if she had been ripped right out of a 1950s sit-com script.

The only words the Scelfo children didn't want to hear from their mother was, "Go see your father." Sometimes it was the belt, but Sam's favorite method of punishment was a backhand across the chest. Discipline was never lacking in the Scelfo family, whether on or off the field.

At age 13, Chris was tossed from a baseball game by his dad. Taking his warm-up tosses before the game, Chris apparently lacked the needed focus. Sam thought he was goofing off, and as the team's coach, he didn't stutter. He told his son to go sit on the team bus, where Chris sat slumped until the game was over. It didn't matter that it was an important game in an important tournament, one that the team had traveled all the way to Texas play in.

In another key baseball game, the lesson Sam taught his son was a bit different. Chris was pitching a marvelous game. With his team tied 1-1 in the late innings, Chris was called for a questionable balk; that runner eventually scored, and his team lost, 2-1. After the game, Sam pulled aside his son. Staring at him with a familiar intensity, Sam sighed deeply, placing his hand on his son's shoulder: "It wasn't your fault we lost. We will learn from it and get over this," he told Chris in a comforting tone.

For Sam Scelfo, there were always lessons to be learned. That much has carried over to Chris Scelfo, the coach. Life is third and long. Attack, attack, attack: to be successful one has to approach every task with a purpose. But lying under that lesson is another one his dad made sure to impart: learn, and teach, perspective.

Some years later, in 1999, his Tulane team was locked in a thriller with conference rival Alabama-Birmingham. The score was knotted at 20-20 on Tulane's final drive of regulation. With the clock winding down, Tulane's freshman kicker Seth Marler attempted a 34-yard field goal that sailed wide right. The game went into overtime, and suddenly Marler was back on the Superdome turf for a second crucial field-goal attempt. This one was blocked. On the ensuing possession, Alabama-Birmingham converted a field goal, ending the game and the season for Tulane. Coach Scelfo quickly found his dejected kicker on the sideline, tears crawling toward the kid's chinstrap. Putting his arm around Marler, Chris repeated his father's message from years ago; this was not his fault, and there would be plenty more football to play.

Two years later, Marler won the Lou Groza Award, given to the nation's best college kicker. By 2003, he would be kicking in the NFL.

○ ○ ○

Years before Chris Scelfo would become the Tulane football coach, he was one of the school's biggest football fans. His older brother, also named Sam, played ball at Tulane, and it was Chris' dream to play on the Green Wave offensive line. Tulane recruited him, sending an assistant to a game in which Chris had played well, but they were not impressed. Soon came a phone call and a rejection: Chris wasn't "big enough" to play for Tulane. His father consoled him, igniting him with a passion to prove Tulane wrong. So Chris took the next best scholarship offer from Northeast Louisiana.

It was there that the red-shirt freshman lineman on the football team sat in his dorm room listening to his sister tell him by phone that his father had passed away. It was there that he was forced to grapple with all sorts of emotions, namely the one telling him to quit football and go home to be with his family; to care for his mother; to deal with the loss of a man who had driven him to always do his best. But after the funeral, Sydney wouldn't let him stay home, and his older brothers threatened to "kick his butt" if he gave any more thought to dropping out of school.

Chris had one more reason to gut it out, and it was a good one: Nancy Caldwell, a student at Northeast Louisiana. The romance—which hardly had the makings of Rhett and Scarlet—began on a Saturday night. A mutual friend, Helene Abraham, introduced Chris to Nancy. She was cute, but their conversation lasted only seconds. The two promptly drifted back toward their respective friends, and that was that—until a Mardi Gras celebration that spring. Nancy and Helene met Chris and a friend in Lafayette, Louisiana. There, they took in a parade, and afterward the boys hitched a ride back to campus in Helene's car.

Chris sat in the backseat with Nancy, and in a move straight out of the This-Is-Why-You're-Single handbook, he went in headfirst for a kiss. An embarrassed Nancy pushed him away, and an equally embarrassed Chris called her a name. The cocksure freshman had a thing or two to learn about dating.

A few months later, the Clark Gable of Northeast Louisiana was at a gas station when he spotted Nancy. Chris hadn't talked to her since the backseat debacle, but he was dogged, so he engaged her in some small talk. That conversation went better than his first two attempts, and with a slight boost of confidence, he asked Nancy for her telephone number. Reluctantly, she wrote it down. Remembering those lessons about earning what his heart desired, Chris called Nancy every night in the hopes of making up lost ground.

With each late-night chat, Nancy's guard lowered. Chris was kind of funny. Cute, too. And a football player to boot. That summer of 1982, the pair remained in Monroe, sharing nights together at the pool hall or pizza parlor. Soon, Chris had made up his mind: it was time for Nancy to sit on the hot seat and meet his parents. The good ol' Southern girl did just fine as Sam Scelfo introduced her to the fine art of peeling crawfish.

Just a few months later, that fall, Sam Scelfo died. But his son, Chris, remained enrolled at Northeast Louisiana, despite the self-described "fog" of emptiness and hopelessness he was often lost in. Then, on April 27, 1983, nearly seven months after his father had died, Chris' brother called with more bad news: their mother was in the hospital.

Chris and Nancy hopped in her orange Volkswagen and headed south to New Iberia. At a gas station just north of Alexandria, Louisiana, Chris called home to check in. His mother had suffered a heart attack and had died. "According to the doctors," Chris remembers, "my mother's was more of a broken heart."

For the second time that year, he pulled his father's stiff sport coat off a closet hanger and buried a parent. Sydney Scelfo rested by her husband's side, leaving Chris a parentless 19-year-old with nothing but questions.

After the funeral, after the continuous hugs from strangers and squeezes from siblings, after the drive back to Monroe that seemed to take an eternity, after kissing Nancy goodnight, Chris sprawled onto his bed and bawled himself to sleep, a feeling of loneliness gnawing at his gut. The fog he found himself lost in after his father's death refused to lift that school year. He made it through finals—somehow—and remained in the dorms over the summer, by himself. He had decisions to make.

"During that time right there," Chris recalls, "I determined I wanted to be somebody. All of the other stuff—the feeling sorry for myself, the 'Why me's,' the things that for seven months I'd been blaming everything on—had to stop." He developed a new sort of tunnel vision, a maniacal determination to succeed. He mapped out his life and set course. Step by step, he would carry on his parents' proud legacy. Chris became stronger in the weight room, then achieved a starting spot on the offensive line and the title of team captain. He graduated, and then earned his master's degree in education. In his personal life, he devoted himself to Nancy, becoming a loving boyfriend.

But his eyes were set on one ultimate goal: becoming a football coach. In the fall of 1986, the Northeast Louisiana graduate and former team captain became a graduate assistant, coaching the offensive linemen he had called his teammates just 12 months prior. Chris loved beating the sun up in the morning and knowing it had set while he sat cramped in a film session, studying strategy, dissecting an opposing defense's nuances and tearing them apart.

In the winter off-season following his first year as a grad assistant, Scelfo began an annual tradition of traveling to a national coaches' convention to shake the hand of every man older than himself. By his own admission, he definitely made the All-Lobby Team. That effort led to his big break, when he landed the ultimate in graduate assistant gigs at the University of Oklahoma under wildly successful coach Barry Switzer.

All Switzer did was coach in big games, winning the national championship in 1985 and finishing No. 3 in the nation the following two years. In his two seasons at Oklahoma, Chris soaked up Switzer's knowledge and passion the same way he had soaked up his dad's. It didn't take him long to realize that successful coaching at the college level was far more than just Xs and Os.

Chris' vision of his life was taking shape. He married Nancy in 1987, and soon followed Oklahoma assistant coach Jim Donnan to Division I-AA Marshall University. Under Donnan, Chris coached the offensive line for six years and coordinated the offense for three. His offensive strategy was innovative and pass-happy, a coaching gumbo of Switzer strategy and Sam Scelfo intensity. In Chris' six years at Marshall, the Thundering Herd played for the national championship four times, winning once. In 1996, Donnan left to fill an opening at the University of Georgia; he took Chris with him, and promoted him to assistant head coach at the tender age of 32.

Two years later, Tulane came knocking, hoping to snag an up-and-coming coach for its program; the offensive lineman once deemed too small to play for them was now too hot to pass up. Both the universities of Louisiana-Lafayette and Louisiana-Monroe—Chris' alma mater—also offered him their head coaching jobs. But Chris was set on Tulane.

When coach Tommy Bowden left the undefeated Green Wave for Clemson in December of 1998, Tulane snatched up the 35-year-old coach.

Just weeks after his hire, Coach Scelfo led the team to a victory against Brigham Young University in the Liberty Bowl, capping off Tulane's undefeated season. Chris and his oldest brother, Frank, now Tulane's offensive coordinator, planned a pass-first offense around new starting quarterback Patrick Ramsey. The plan harkened back to the frontyard exploits the brothers had shared as children growing up in Sam Scelfo's home, except now, the neighborhood kids had been replaced by NFL prospects.

But beyond the Xs and Os, Chris led by example, offering his players a father figure they could place their faith in. Ramsey's successor and a current NFL quarterback, J. P. Losman, said he always knew that no matter what obstacles he faced on or off the football field, that Coach Scelfo's advice would always be true.

Providing his players with that support was just part of Scelfo's role as head coach. First, he had to convince those same players to join him at Tulane. That was an important lesson he had learned from shadowing superb recruiter Barry Switzer at Oklahoma.

Scelfo relied on his instinct, remembering what had made his own parents tick when it came to deciding which school was right for their children. His pitch was simple: "Come to Tulane, and you will leave a college graduate." It was the company line in college recruiting, but when recruiting kids from schools whose valedictorians couldn't spell valedictorian, it still carried weight.

Linebacker Brandon Spincer echoes that sentiment. A dominant defender for New Orleans' St. Augustine High, Spincer said the key to his recruitment was convincing his parents, not him. Scelfo delivered his pitch just as if he was speaking to his own parents. "On Saturdays your son will be on display at the Superdome," he told them, "and four years later, he'll be back at the Superdome walking down the aisle in a cap and gown."

Spincer recalled: "I looked up at my mom, and she was all smiles, nodding her head. He had my parents, so he had me."

At times during the exhausting recruiting process, a recruit becomes more of a statistic—a sought-after conquest—than an impressionable soul. But once a recruit signs that dotted line for Coach Scelfo, evolution occurs instantly: the recruit becomes Chris' kin.

"Coach talks about us being like his own children," quarterback Lester Ricard said. "I truly believe that."

But like every paternal relationship, there is sometimes rebellion and struggle. Chris was greeted by a belt too many times as a child to forget this truth. With Spincer, first came the frustration—the kid didn't live up to his end of the bargain, and became academically ineligible in 2002—followed by the rebellion—Spincer wanted to play safety, and Scelfo needed him at linebacker. But by 2005, when Spincer was a senior and back at linebacker, the evolutionary process had taken an unforeseen step forward. Spincer hadn't just evolved into Scelfo's "kin." The player had evolved into the spitting image of Scelfo: a proud, determined, hard-nosed man; a team captain; a father of two.

Spincer's maturation happened at the right time, when his team and his coach needed his leadership the most. When Hurricane Katrina smacked into the Gulf Coast, Spincer was suddenly cast in a new role. "That storm really brought me and Coach Scelfo closer," Spincer said, "as coach and player and man to man. Some things got overwhelming, but I watched him handle the situation, and it was like a life lesson for me. The one thing that I've learned from Coach is perseverance. I didn't know what the meaning of perseverance was [until that storm hit]. . . . He would pull me to the side and tell me: you have to be a leader. I really stayed strong through that whole ordeal by feeding off of him."

What would happen next in Coach Scelfo's life, as his frightened football team evacuated to Dallas, had no precedence. Sam Scelfo had taught his son perseverance, and in turn Chris Scelfo was teaching his kin the meaning of the word. But this was a new challenge. No diagram of Xs and Os could prepare him for coaching perseverance in the wake of Katrina.

CHAPTER 5

Dallas

$\mathcal{I}$n Dallas, the reality of what the team had caught a glimpse of on the Shreveport truck stop TV finally set in. In the Dallas Doubletree lobby, Coach Scelfo sat parked in front of a bar television tuned to CNN. It was Wednesday, the team's first day in its new temporary home at the Doubletree Inn. Coach watched his players walk slowly past him, uncertain and frightened, lost in their own fog. He'd overheard more than one player grumble, "I don't give a s--- about anything." Scelfo knew exactly what they meant, having trekked down that slippery path himself as a young man. He recalled the fog of his youth, the uncertainty and despair that followed the death of his parents, and knew the current emotions coursing through him were all too familiar.

But sitting in front of that television, Scelfo faced a new sort of challenge. His kin needed him. His players were homeless; this was the exact moment he had promised so many parents that he would come through for their kids—when they needed him most. It was time to coach, not mope. And so Scelfo began to strategize a plan of attack to defeat an opponent he had never faced before, had no game tape of, and could never actually wrestle to the ground. The one thing he had going for him were those lessons he had learned on perseverance. In his words, he felt he could give the team something it would need in the coming dark days—a pair of headlights.

○ ○ ○

Linebackers Brandon Spincer and Anthony Cannon spent Wednesday cooped in their hotel room. Normally, the two would be sitting side by side in film sessions, watching the frame-by-frame movements of their opponent's offensive stars; this day, however, they sat next to each other, fixated on Anderson Cooper. On CNN, Cannon spotted a Shell gas station sign peeking from the floodwaters in Uptown New Orleans. Then he saw a well-known Walgreens. This was his street corner, he determined, and when the camera showed the street signs—Claiborne and Napoleon—his worst fears were displayed in living color. The apartment he shared with teammate and best friend Sean Lucas was right around the corner from that drug store. And Tulane University was just a mile down Claiborne.

Spincer soon had a similar revelation. The screen zoomed in on another section of town, where the floodwaters had slammed through the levees and into civilization. "I know that building," Spincer told Cannon, soon realizing why he knew it: it was close to his old stomping grounds at St. Augustine High School. "I saw the level of water, and that's when I realized it was way worse than I had thought," Spincer said. A panic set in. He had established contact with his parents, who were staying with his grandparents in Greenville, Mississippi, and his two children were safe with their mother in Houston. But despite his efforts, he could not reach his 21-year-old brother, Christopher. All that was left to do was ponder his brother's health, eyes continually fixed on CNN as day gave way to night and eventually morning. Spincer had grown up in a tough part of town; poverty was not something he was unfamiliar with. But after taking in hour after hour of television footage displaying the desperation of a post-Katrina New Orleans, Spincer was shell-shocked. "That's where *I* live?" he muttered aloud. "It's worse than a third-world country."

Christopher was supposed to be staying at the Fairmont Hotel in downtown New Orleans, but was there even a Fairmont Hotel anymore? Spincer, like so many other teammates, had been taken hostage by doubt.

Lester Ricard, the preacher's son, watched the hours pass on the hotel alarm clock. He was waiting to hear word of his great uncle Edward, who had chosen to weather the storm at his home in New Orleans' Ninth Ward. Ricard feared the worst and spent his first day in the Doubletree praying. Wednesday gave way to Thursday, and Ricard still had not heard whether his uncle was alive.

Others had heard, and the news was not good. Bubba Terranova walked into his hotel room and there, on the bed, sat his teammate and fellow Louisianan, Kenneth Guidroz. In one hand Guidroz was holding a phone, while his other hand busied itself wiping away tears. "They found my uncles dead," Guidroz told Terranova. The two sat on the bed, silent, sobbing. The following day, Guidroz received another call—inexplicably, his uncles had survived. But now his father, Kenneth Sr., was missing. Later that same day, Guidroz received word that his father had survived the storm as well. He took a deep breath and forced a smile. His hometown of Port Sulpher, Louisiana, had been obliterated by the storm, but his family had survived.

The sadness was too much for a kid to bear, but the adults had no easier time processing the chaos and confusion. Each click of the remote control was like a slug to the stomach of Tulane assistant coach Garret Chachere, every image of New Orleans a blow landed squarely to his body. There were his people, his neighbors, trapped. In the coming days, he would receive many phone calls from random cell numbers, as friends and family dialed him to tell him news of evacuations, of near-misses, of tragedies. Sitting in the Doubletree lobby, dark semi-circles under his eyes, Chachere related a story of a call he had received from a close friend whose father had lost his business to the flood. Days later, the friend would call back to say his father had died, succumbing to a heart attack. Calls like that kept coming.

Chachere was quick to point out what so many failed to understand: standing in those long lines at the Superdome and the Convention Center weren't just the city's poor or homeless; Chachere knew plenty of common folks just like him who were left stranded on Interstate 10. Reality was that Katrina's reach stretched farther than CNN was letting on.

o   o   o

Since the team's arrival in Dallas, Coach Scelfo had assumed the roles of surrogate father, therapist, motivational speaker, and CEO. While he was far from his players' sole motivator, he was an anchor for each to latch onto. And he was functioning on next-to-no sleep—one hour a night maybe. Over the coming days, he would bounce from meetings to practice to meetings, sustaining himself on a diet of coffee, caffeine, and hugs from his family, who had all joined the team at the Doubletree. Having his family around was a blessing, but it only made the hole in his players' lives more obvious. Many were missing their families badly, even as good news began to slowly sift in. No Tulane player had lost a family member, despite some close calls.

It's hardly fair to compare the suffering of a displaced football team to that of an entire city, especially when members of that city were trapped in flooded attics or suffering from inhumane conditions at the Superdome. But Coach Scelfo's team was symbolic of the plight that faced all those modest, working-class families who were lucky enough to escape New Orleans before the storm hit. Their future was weighted down with uncertainty, but more relevant to the situation at hand, the present was also up for grabs. The football team had next-to-nothing: little more in the way of clothing than what they had on their backs when they fled the bayou, and no money (bank accounts throughout New Orleans were frozen). Scelfo worked the phones incessantly, talking to boosters and old friends in the hopes of scrounging up donations for his team. Boxes came by the dozens full of toiletries, football equipment, and clothing. Players may have grumbled about sporting matching T-shirts from the Texas Motor Speedway, but clean clothing was clean clothing.

Scelfo and his staff organized a makeshift locker room and meeting rooms in a ballroom at the hotel. While the Southern Miss game had been postponed until November, their next scheduled game against Mississippi State on September 17 was the target return date. So the team began to prepare for the Bulldogs, even though their scouting tapes were floating in New Orleans.

The challenges to getting ready for the game presented themselves immediately; Tulane's football team had more pressing concerns than exploiting the Bulldogs defense, namely finding a home where it could hole up for the season. Surely, it wasn't going to be the lobby of the Dallas Doubletree. Working with school officials, Scelfo considered several options before deciding on Ruston, Louisiana, the home of Louisiana Tech University, as a realistic possibility. The logistics of such a move, including class enrollment and the need for training facilities, produced a headache too mighty for Advil. Throughout it all, Scelfo had to maintain his team's focus and sense of perspective. Sure their situation was less than ideal, but it could have been a lot worse. "Just turn on the TV," he told his team. "That's our motivation. We're not just representing ourselves and the university. We're representing the whole city."

"I don't understand how Coach did it," said offensive lineman Michael Parenton. "There's no precedent to say, 'He should have done it this way or that way.' I think that was the toughest part of his job from the beginning. He had 87 kids. Everything he did was not going to please all 87. . . . To be flung into that position, how could you honestly criticize him?"

The press was hardly looking for someone to criticize, however. They had the story of a century on their hands. Tulane sports information director John Sudsbury, stationed in Dallas with the team, sent a simple text message to the *Times-Picayune* beat writer on Wednesday morning: "Call me at this number if you need to do a story."

By that Wednesday night, the *Times-Picayune* had sent a staff writer to the Dallas Doubletree, who would spend every waking moment with the players and coaches. Before Katrina struck, the final story in the August 28 issue of the *Times-Picayune* about Tulane football was a fluffy piece on the defense. The next story in the *Times-Picayune* about Tulane football—at that point available only on the newspaper's website, as the paper was not being circulated in a print version—ran with the headline: "Team tries to come to grips as reality, possibility swirl."

In those first days in Dallas, numerous major newspapers sent reporters to write stories about a team on the run. Headlines popped up across North America: "All we have now is football," wrote the *Los Angeles Times*; "Tulane hungry to play," said the *Miami Herald*; "Tulane counts its blessings; winning doesn't matter anymore," reported the *Winnipeg Sun*. Little Tulane of Conference USA was the biggest story in college football—sometimes for wrong and unfortunate reasons.

Normally, Sudsbury was nudging the local New Orleans media to cover the Green Wave; now he was inundated, a cell phone in both palms, turning down calls from international journalists and letting the *New York Times* go to voicemail. ESPN sent a crew to the Doubletree, where cameras zoomed in on tears and reporters asked point-blank questions like, "What's it like to lose your home?" to a 19-year-old who didn't know how to put such emotions into a sound bite.

Tulane was New Orleans' only college football team. After Katrina, Tulane's story was, in the minds of the national media, perfectly poignant, a splash of sports, a fresh angle in the wake of disaster. Sure, there were the NFL's Saints and the NBA's Hornets, New Orleans sports teams-turned-evacuees. Of course, both teams became beacons of their city in the coming months. But those professional athletes could buy another home with last month's salary. Most of the Tulane athletes who had lost their family homes would never play professionally, and their rebuilding process would be anything but easy.

Neighboring Louisiana State University was a pretty good story, too. Many of its players were Louisiana-bred and had ties to New Orleans. And they were the No. 5 team in the country at the time. So the Bayou Bengals became mainstays on *SportsCenter*, celebrated in the pages of *Sports Illustrated*. "That's the media for you," Spincer said. "That's Louisiana's team. They're going to get exposure. But they didn't go through what we went through. I know guys on that team, and they told me that. They know."

LSU still had their campus, their training facilities, their football stadium. What Tulane was going through that Wednesday afternoon was an introduction to their new practice field at Dallas' Jesuit High School. Here, the team would practice. But practice for what? The Tulane squad was still uncertain as to whether or not there would even be a football season. Exhausted, sleep-deprived, and scared, the players didn't even know if there would be a Tulane to represent when the floodwaters subsided.

Coach Scelfo understood their concern. But the point of this practice wasn't to perfect a no-huddle offense; it was to provide his crew with some much-needed therapy. He wanted his players to lose themselves on the field in drill after drill because football, hopefully, could comfort them. "Quite simply," Scelfo told his staff, "when you're thinking about football, you ain't thinking about Katrina."

What happened that sunny afternoon was amazing: Scelfo had never been part of a more focused practice. His ragged, emotional team gave him a gut-wrenching, heartwarming performance. "So much had been going on for me that was not in my comfort zone," Scelfo said. "But walking onto that field, I was in my comfort zone. The field was the same size as it was back home; the kids were running around. For two hours I wasn't going through hell."

The team's second practice on the high school field was less focused, partly thanks to hovering camera crews. It was now Thursday, September 1, another gorgeous day in Dallas. Whistles pierced the air. Coach Scelfo roared at his players during drills. Sudsbury stood on the sideline on his cell phone. Spincer caught himself daydreaming, wondering what his brother was doing at that moment, trapped in New Orleans.

Terranova, the receiver from Slidell, wafted through practice drills. Tragedy had smothered his life, and the pressure of such loss was building inside him. His mother, who he spoke with daily via phone, encouraged him to talk about how he was feeling, but he'd tell her in his low voice, "I don't really express myself."

That afternoon during practice, the pressure finally burst: Terranova tried to catch a pass between defenders. Then, suddenly he was throwing punches at safety Tra Boger. After calming everyone down, Scelfo gently put his arm on Terranova's shoulder pads. The receiver quietly told him, "We lost everything. And my mom, she's not doing well."

Scelfo looked deep into Terranova's frightened eyes. He told his player that it was natural to react to difficult emotions. But it couldn't spill onto the practice field. It couldn't shake the team. All they had was the team. Terranova thanked Scelfo for his words, hugged him, and then jogged to the bus.

That night, the team was invited to the Dallas Cowboys pre-season game against the Jacksonville Jaguars as guests of Cowboys owner Jerry Jones. At that point, donations had yet to pour in, so the only clothes the players had were T-shirts and shorts. Scelfo called up Tulane booster Jim Wilson Jr., who arranged for the team to purchase some appropriate clothing at a nearby store. But Dickson, the athletic director, called Scelfo just as the players were browsing the racks and told him that such purchases were against NCAA rules. Scelfo was furious; his football team had been turned into a band of evacuees, and the administration was worried about the legality of purchasing jeans?

Before 2005, Dickson thought he had seen it all. In the spring of 2003, the passionate athletic director's program was put under review by Tulane University. There was a legitimate chance that the program, financially strapped and competing in a non-Bowl Championship Series conference, would be dropped to Division III by the Tulane Board. That level of college athletics does not grant scholarships and is financially easier to run. Dickson emerged as a hero that spring, spearheading a fundraising campaign to save his program and his job.

Now here he was in 2005, trying to coordinate the future of his program once again. This time, he had his teams scattered at universities across the south. He needed to enroll every student-athlete in another university while keeping the teams together, schedule game venues, reschedule games that had been postponed by the hurricane, find his disbanded support staff, determine how many millions of dollars of damage had occurred on Tulane's campus and, in the midst of all these other challenges, try to make sure the team didn't get into any trouble by breaking rules.

Dickson's passion was equal to Scelfo's; Dickson's, though, was for maintaining an entire athletic program, whereas Scelfo's was solely for the immediate well-being of his football players. Eventually, the two men and the NCAA worked out the kinks with the clothing purchases, and a Tulane athletic booster named James Wilson Jr. arranged for the players to return to the store.

That Thursday night, Tulane sat in the stands at the Cowboys game. Scelfo, his mind swirling with tasks, was stuck: he *had* to just sit there and relax. But when he left his seat to use the bathroom, he spotted a player at the bathroom faucet, leaning over the sink, cupping water in his hands. Scelfo realized what was happening; the player didn't have any money to buy a drink. None of his players had any money on them. These kids were his responsibility entirely.

Scelfo clenched his jaw and returned to his seat, fidgeting through the final quarters. On the bus back, the coach spoke feverishly to his team, asking if anyone could have money wired in from out of town. Senior Lyneal Strain was able to get $50 for each player.

"From that point on," Scelfo says, "I wasn't worried about any rules because there wasn't one thing I was going to do that I couldn't justify." Whatever needed to be done, Scelfo would find a way to do it.

CHAPTER 6

Brothers

No Tulane player emblemized the city of New Orleans more than Tulane's soulful, fiercely proud linebacker, Brandon Spincer. A New Orleans-native, Spincer was the heart of the Tulane defense. He stood 6-feet-2, 213 pounds, with arms so chiseled he could seemingly slice bread with his triceps.

Spincer grew up in Uptown New Orleans, the historic area that is home to the Tulane campus. There, Saint Charles Avenue crawls through the city, lined with glorious oak trees and mansions big enough to have their own zip codes. Residents of this area dine at Clancy's and Upperline, some of the finest restaurants in the country, and their homes are just a golf cart's trek away from the magnificently green Audubon Park golf course.

But this is not Spincer's Uptown. New Orleans, perhaps more than any other city in the country, is a checkerboard of wealth and poverty. Pockets of Uptown New Orleans are plagued with crime and despair. Right off of Saint Charles Avenue is Hillary Street, where the homes decrease in size and value as one travels just a few hundred yards down. This is Spincer's neighborhood: "The UPT," or as some of its residents call it, "Niggatown."

Shootings were common in the area. "Before the storm happened that summer, at least 10 people I knew got killed," said Christopher Spincer, Brandon's brother. "In a way, it was good that Katrina happened, because if not, then a lot more people that I know probably would be dead."

Brandon Spincer had both parents in his life, a rarity in his neighborhood. His childhood memories were filled with a combination of hope and hopelessness, as well as piercing lessons from his parents and many images of anguish. His childhood friends had older brothers in gangs. Neighborhood kids dealt drugs like kids elsewhere traded baseball cards. One night, the 15-year-old Brandon was watching television when gunshots echoed on his street. Then sirens. Shivering, he peeked out the front door. On the street was a murdered drug dealer, dying near the spot where he usually played ball with his friends.

○ ○ ○

Once, as his father played cards with some friends, Brandon sneaked under his father's chair. Suddenly, he lifted the chair—with his father still in it. Brandon was six years old at the time. His strength became known throughout the neighborhood, on the playground, and eventually on the football field. Christopher remembers sitting in the tattered bleachers at his brother's youth football games, watching his brother steamroll tacklers like dominoes. Their mother, Barbara, would have to bring Brandon's birth certificate to youth football games just to prove to opposing coaches that Brandon was the same age as that coach's players.

At St. Augustine High, Brandon was a hallway hero. Football powerhouses such as the University of Colorado sent letters to Hillary Street. But Brandon, who became a father to Branisha when he was just 17, yearned to stay in New Orleans. Soon he met Coach Scelfo. The bond was instant. Brandon would fulfill his dreams of playing college football just two miles from his home.

As a freshman for Tulane, he started immediately, making 65 tackles in 2001. As a freshman *at* Tulane, he struggled in his transition from a poor New Orleans High School to the highly ranked university. In 2002, he became academically ineligible.

After working hard in the classroom, Spincer returned to the field in 2003, notching 63 tackles. He then moved from linebacker to safety in 2004; he decided he'd have a better chance of going pro at that position. It was a failed experiment. In spring practice of 2005, he moved back to linebacker, and by August he was a hulking, grizzled force in the middle of Tulane's budding defense.

But there he was, days into September, at the Dallas Doubletree, feeling alone among teammates. Instead of thinking about his next game, he was worried about his brother, Christopher. He hadn't heard from him since August.

Christopher had always wanted to be just like Brandon. Two grades younger, he would sit in the stands at Brandon's St. Augustine games and watch his brother desecrate offenses. People would approach Christopher at school the next Monday, their eyes as wide as silver dollars, and say, "Did you see that hit Brandon made?" Football made his brother an idol, and going to college made him someone to emulate.

But Brandon was a role model off the field, too. He would lecture his little brother about perseverance, as if he himself were a football coach. He would tell Christopher stories: about his friends who quit football and joined gangs; about his own struggles through academic ineligibility; about his focus in the weight room, where the 10th bench press was the one that made a man, not the first nine; about being a kid with a kid, and how fatherhood was something to cherish.

Christopher would absorb these talks, say, "Thanks," and go about his way. But privately, Christopher said to himself, "He's a great brother, a great friend, and he's a hero. And if he's not a hero to anybody else, he's a hero to me."

In early August of 2005, Christopher enrolled in Jackson State, where Tulane would spend its first nights of evacuation later in the month. A few days prior to Katrina, even before the hurricane began brewing, Christopher and his parents had packed their car and driven three hours north. Christopher didn't know what he wanted to be in life, except, of course, he wanted to be like Brandon. "I've always looked up to him, but I don't ever tell him. He already has a big head," he said. Brandon was on pace to get his college degree.

But when Christopher arrived at Jackson State, his financial aid did not cover all their expenses, and his attempts to get loans fell through. Despite their hopes that Christopher would be able to enroll in classes, the Spincers got back in the car and drove south, back to New Orleans.

Later that week, a forlorn Christopher first heard about Hurricane Katrina. Initially, he wrote the storm off: Here we go again, he thought. Every summer, one of these tropical teases comes along, and we waste another day in highway gridlock, evacuating to Mississippi, only to turn around and return to an untouched New Orleans the next week.

Even though they doubted the storm would affect them, Spincer's parents still decided to drive to Greenville, Mississippi, where his grandparents lived. Christopher wasn't interested in making the trip. If the endless hours in traffic weren't discouraging enough, Christopher had no desire to drive back into Mississippi just days after his depressing drive there. Also, his best friend, Wilfred "Buut" Griffin, was going to spend the weekend in New Orleans' Fairmont Hotel, on the fringe of French Quarter, to celebrate his mother's upcoming birthday (she would be 55 on August 29). Buut's parents, Wilfred Sr. and Gilda, were Christopher's godparents, and Wilfred worked at the Fairmont. So instead of driving to Mississippi, Christopher figured he'd spend the time at the Fairmont with the Griffin family in the hopes that it would take his mind off his frustrations.

Christopher showed up on Saturday the 27th with a small bag containing a couple pairs of shorts, a couple T-shirts and tank tops, some socks, and underwear. When they got to the hotel, though, the boys found out they would only have one room—and one bed. The room was on the ninth floor, and there were five of them staying there: Christopher and Buut; Buut's parents, Wilfred and Gilda; and Gilda's sister, Jenny, who was wheelchair-bound.

Buut brought some video games, so the boys played Madden and talked trash. They slipped off to the weight room to get in a lift. They watched the movie *Hitch*, the playful story about a surefire ladies' man who lost his groove when he met his dream girl.

Outside, the wind slowly began to swirl. By Sunday, Christopher had an ominous feeling. People were talking about

Katrina in a way they hadn't talked about other hurricanes. In other instances, by this time, people had received word that a looming hurricane had lost steam or died in the gulf. But Katrina kept clawing. Christopher waited in his cot, wondering if New Orleans could possibly be in for a direct hit.

On Monday morning, August 29, 2005—Gilda's birthday—Christopher woke up around 10 a.m. The room was dark. The power was out. Buut and his father were still sleeping. Gilda and her sister were in front of the large windowpane, fixated on the waterfall of rain slapping the window. Wind sent leaves and other debris swirling around downtown. In the distance they could see that the windows on other buildings were smashed.

"This is the hurricane," Christopher said, joining them at the window. "I mean, we're actually *in* the hurricane."

Once the rain stopped that Monday, Christopher and Buut walked outside onto Canal Street, the well-known street that divided the Central Business District with the French Quarter. Dozens of other people from hotels wandered onto Canal Street, too, where they walked in dizzying circles, absorbing the destruction. Cars were smashed into the sides of buildings. Debris littered the streets. The tourists' Mecca was a disaster zone.

Christopher spotted a buddy who had photographed the Hyatt, the hotel near the Superdome in the Central Business District. He showed Christopher photos of the hotel, dozens of windows punched in. The checkered façade looked like a crossword puzzle. In front, a tattered American flag hung from a pole. Christopher began to hear stories about the Superdome. Just like the Tulane players in the Jackson gym, no one knew for sure what was happening. But rumors grew with each telling. As night fell, police began to patrol Canal Street, advising people to return to their hotels. There was still a semblance of control.

On Tuesday, Buut was the first one up. He walked down to the lobby, but had to turn around and take the steps back up to the ninth floor. There was still no electricity, so it was candle-light that revealed his bewildered face as he reported what he'd seen: Canal Street, he said, was now a river. In their room, they had a small television that ran on batteries, so they watched scratchy footage of water flowing through the streets of New Orleans like a Mardi Gras parade. The storm surge had over-whelmed the floodwalls, which had previously protected New Orleans from massive floodwaters during storms. On this day, the levees broke.

Christopher could see the panic in his godmother's eyes. Everyone in the room lived near the levees. She trembled in her seat. She was always the one to go to for support when times were rough, but on this day, she could not stop crying. They only had a handful of necessities in the stuffy hotel room. The hotel had a generator running downstairs, and they supplied guests with sandwiches, fruits, and other foods that would soon go bad because of the lack of refrigeration.

Christopher was with his godparents, but this was one of those times where he yearned for his own parents. And he missed his brother, the rock in his life. Things were never that bad when Brandon was in Christopher's corner. Without his family close by, the hours passed even more slowly.

On Wednesday, desperate and delirious, Buut went down to Canal Street and waded through the waist-high water. He fol-lowed resourceful masses into a Walgreens, which they looted for necessities; he also followed people into a Foot Locker, which they looted because they could. Buut returned to the room and tossed Christopher a new pair of shoes. Christopher just shook his head in disappointment.

On Thursday, New Orleans was just as sunny as it was in Dallas. That afternoon, while Brandon Spincer practiced football at Jesuit High, Christopher Spincer rested on his hotel cot in the darkness. His godfather walked in asked him for a little help; they needed some supplies, and he needed an extra set of hands. Christopher peered up from his cot with a scowl. There was no way he would participate in the looting, not with the police threatening looters with rifles, not with people drowning.

But his godfather was persistent. He had been out there before—Christopher hadn't. There was no word as to when any relief was coming, and the situation was becoming desperate. They needed some supplies—Gilda had trouble breathing—and Walgreens was just around the corner. Christopher sighed and slowly got out of the cot, hoping the mattress would suck him back into safety.

Out on the street, scattered heads and shoulders bobbed up and down, wading through the flood, their weary arms filled with loot. Christopher saw people battling to stay above water while carrying televisions. Where, he thought to himself, were they possibly going to plug in that television in a powerless city?

The doors at the Walgreens were locked, but a window had already been smashed in. Christopher and his godfather crawled into the store, ducking into the smashed hole, splattering water inside with each sweeping step through. It was dark inside the store, and the sunrays created eerie shadows along the damp walls. As he approached one of the aisles, Christopher heard faint noises. His heart had already been racing—now, it was pounding. He tiptoed around the corner, dreading what he might see.

It was a man looting. Christopher took a deep breath, still not believing he was participating in the same crime. He started collecting bottles of water and Red Bull, the energy drink. Christopher was in the back of the store; his godfather was in the front. At least, Christopher thought, at least we'll be out of here soon. He grabbed another bottle.

Suddenly, there was a commotion from the front of the store. "Put that fucking shit down!" someone screamed. Frozen, Christopher looked around the corner. There were two men dressed in all black. They seemed to be police officers. One was pointing an M-16 at his godfather. "Put the shit down!"

Christopher and Wilfred, their bodies seized by a cold fright, threw the water and supplies to the ground. But the other looter, a Mexican-American man, didn't understand English. He was in the back of the store and couldn't see the gun. All he heard was indecipherable screaming. One of the officers kept his gun pointed at Wilfred even after he dropped the items. The other policeman, without his gun showing, walked slowly toward the back of the store and spotted the third man, who was corralling a garbage bag filled with supplies.

"Put it down, or I'm going to shoot you!" the officer screamed.

"No English," the confused man said. "No English!" he repeated. The cop whipped out his gun, and the man dropped the garbage bag. "Y'all get the fuck out of here!" the other officer screamed.

The cops waited for the three men at the smashed window. Christopher's godfather began walking towards them, obeying their commands. As he ducked under the broken glass to leave, one of the officers grabbed the back of his shirt and pushed him down into the floodwaters, which splashed as Wilfred was thrown in. Rising after a moment, now drenched, he gathered himself outside the store, waiting for his young godson.

Now it was Christopher's turn to approach the window. The same officer grabbed his shirt, but Christopher freed himself from his grip to avoid the same shove his godfather had been given. He jumped through the window's hole, away from the deserted store and into the floodwaters. Quickly, he and Wilfred made their way back to the others waiting for them at the hotel.

After wading through the now-flooded lobby and climbing the nine flights of stairs to get back to his room, Christopher dried himself off; the showers were inoperable. He sat back on the cot, his heart still fluttering, when the phone rang—something it hadn't done since the storm hit.

Hundreds of miles away, at the Dallas Doubletree, Brandon had become increasingly anxious as the hours had passed. With each television segment that showed a flooded New Orleans, he worried more and more: How was Christopher? While being interviewed by ESPN, Brandon had desperately asked the production crew to try to get word into New Orleans that his brother had yet to be accounted for. And Coach Scelfo asked reporters to spread word that there were folks stranded in the Fairmont.

At the same instant that his brother had been forced to loot a Walgreens for supplies, Brandon had been in the hotel's business center after that Thursday's practice, scouring the Internet for information about the Fairmont Hotel. He came across its phone number, and though he figured the phones wouldn't be functioning, he dialed anyway. He got no answer. He tried a second number listed on the site despite his increasing hopelessness. After six rings, the miraculous happened: someone picked up.

He explained his situation; he was trying to find his brother, who was with the Griffin family. He was placed on hold for what seemed like an hour as whoever had answered the phone tried to locate the family. And then, after days of having feared the worst, Brandon was finally in contact with his baby brother.

They thanked God that the other was all right and told each other the specifics surrounding what they'd been through during and after the storm. Brandon then used the three-way function on his cell phone to call their mother, who had been desperate to find out if her youngest boy was alive and safe. The family, for a moment, was reunited.

When he hung up the phone, Christopher began to cry. The magnitude of the situation finally hit him: his brother had had to ask television crews to help find him; people were stealing to survive; people were being shot; the streets, normally lined with tourists, were filled with chaos; his parents had feared he was dead. Christopher realized that people watching New Orleans from a distance were filled with overwhelming fear. Through his own eyes, he could finally see the gravity of circumstances they were in. "We got to get out of here," he said out loud.

They wouldn't escape for another two days. On Saturday, September 3—one week after Christopher arrived at the Fairmont—he and the Griffins left New Orleans. A private bus company had arrived to take families out of the city. They were told they were going to Dallas, to stay at the Fairmont there. Christopher carried Jenny, Gilda's wheelchair-bound sister, down the nine slippery flights of stairs and onto the bus. He and Buut helped numerous elderly people out of the building, each person exceedingly helpless and thankful. After assisting others to safety, the boys themselves finally boarded the bus, a week of unfathomable desperation finally behind them.

The bus waded through the New Orleans streets as it inched towards the freeway. The only other signs of life on the streets were military personnel, all of them carrying guns. As the bus rolled slowly across Interstate 10, a beleaguered Christopher peered out the window at the hurricane victims lining the road. Some were dead, their bodies sprawled along the highway's shoulders. The faces haunted him. Scattered among the bodies were mothers holding their children in their arms. Where would these people end up? How would they ever get to safety? The bus, already full, passed them by. The bus also passed the Superdome, once a symbol of the city, now ravaged and symbolic only of Katrina's aftermath. In the distance, the city's buildings were on fire.

More disturbing facts came to light. Soon, they were told that the bus driver had been instructed to take them to Houston, not Dallas. Worse, they were headed for the Houston Astrodome, where Christopher had heard Superdome survivors were being transported, and based on the reports about conditions there, he became worried. Seven hours later, the Greyhound bus pulled towards the Astrodome. It was 8 p.m. Their bus was one in a serpentine line of many, dozens and dozens, each brimming with survivors and their stories. The line was at a complete standstill. In the hours they spent waiting for the line to inch forward, most everyone lingered outside. There, near where Christopher stood, an older woman fell to the ground, suddenly experiencing a seizure. Christopher watched as paramedics arrived and performed CPR on her, furiously pumping her chest. But their efforts came too late, and the woman died just five feet away from Christopher, who watched as they simply put a sheet over her, placed her in an ambulance, and drove off.

As they waited, day turned to night. The evacuees were growing very hungry. Many people still didn't know where their families were, or even if their families were still alive. Frustration manifested itself everywhere; in the parking lot near Christopher, a group of girls began fist fighting. Another man, Christopher had heard, was wandering around like a lunatic. He would walk up the steps of different busses, a maniacal look in his sleepless eyes, and inform mothers to watch their daughters, saying he didn't know what he'd do if he got his hands on one. Christopher and the Griffins remained stalled, chaos brewing around them, unable to shake themselves from this living nightmare.

At around 2 a.m., their bus still a good mile from the Astrodome, Gilda received a call from her other son in Minnesota. He had somehow pulled some strings and arranged for a cab to find their bus and take them to a bus station to get out of town. The family found themselves in an unfamiliar bus station in the middle of the night. There, Christopher devoured some Kentucky Fried Chicken—his first real meal in days—just before saying goodbye to his godparents, Jenny, and his best friend, Buut. They were all headed north to Minnesota; Christopher was headed east to Mississippi.

The trip took all day Sunday. As midnight approached, his bus reached the station near Greenville. The station was closed, so Christopher plopped down on the curb. In the darkness, he recounted the past images: the hurricane's rains pummeling their hotel window; the unstoppable floodwaters; the gun point-ed at Wilfred; the jarring yet welcome sound of the phone ring-ing in their hotel room; the bodies on the side of the highway.

As his mind filled with these images, headlights popped out of the darkness. They zeroed in on Christopher, blinding him for a moment. The car came to a halt. The door opened, and he heard a soothing voice, one he'd been longing to hear: it was his mother's, calling his name.

CHAPTER 7

Family

On Saturday, September 3, the same weekend Tulane had originally been scheduled to play its first game, the Green Wave was forced to sit in the stands. Instead of playing, they attended the SMU Mustangs' game against Baylor. For the team, there was something tormenting about watching a game when they should have been playing in one of their own.

Before the game itself, the Tulane players sifted through the tailgating happening on "The Boulevard" on SMU's campus. The dress code seemed to be business casual. Collars were mandatory, and some exaggerated the mandate by wearing their collars up. Neckties hung loosely from the collars of male students. Others wore polo shirts. The women dressed in designer clothing, as if hoping *Vogue* would stop by for an impromptu photo shoot. The Tulane players, most of them wearing T-shirts, stood out from the fashion show for all the wrong reasons. But they didn't care; they were just glad to be away from the hotel, to be around other students, to get their minds off of Hurricane Katrina.

From the stands during the game, safety Sean Lucas watched SMU safeties break up passes and deliver crunching tackles. His stomach suddenly felt empty, as if he hadn't eaten in a week. Several times as the quarters went by, he said he wanted to leave the game. But he was forced to watch somebody else do what he did best.

Michael Parenton sat next to his best friend, Lester Ricard. For a robust lineman and an austere quarterback, the two were actually a pretty goofy pair. Fun for them was cracking jokes and watching *Batman* into the wee hours. Ricard, who is black, gleefully refers to Parenton, who is white, as his "kin with different skin."

Parenton kept a hand on his cell phone, which rang during the SMU game. The call was from a friend back in New Orleans. Parenton's family lived on Calhoun Street in Uptown, a few football fields away from Tulane's practice football field. Prior to then—specifically, prior to that call—Parenton had handled his emotions regarding the hurricane calmly; he knew his home and school were flooded, but he had a mature perspective on the tragedy. After all, the people he loved were still alive. But the phone call informed Parenton that his family's home had been looted. He sat there, quarantined in Section 211, fuming.

The next day, players gathered in a Doubletree Hotel conference room for a Sunday meeting of the Fellowship of Christian Athletes. Some of the players thought these meetings were phony and unnecessary. Others found them therapeutic and vital. On this afternoon, Lloyd Arnsmeyer, the executive director of the FCA Dallas branch, didn't spew religion in the players' faces. Instead, he emulated Coach Scelfo, speaking of perseverance. He emulated Parenton, Spincer, and others, speaking of perspective.

"You do have life," Arnsmeyer pleaded. "And you do have each other. . . . I don't care what year you are in school, you're going to need help dealing with some issues. . . . Remember, you are a team."

Meanwhile, freshman Jordan Ellis sulked through the time in Dallas. For him, the fog—the fog Coach Scelfo had once waded through years ago, when his parents died—was omnipresent. Long before Katrina hit, during August practices, he'd been very homesick; it was the first time he'd ever been away from his family, and he missed his four siblings. Now, he literally missed his home, presumed gone after the storm. Ellis could not motivate himself. He admitted he did not care about football. So there he was at practices, sulking, floating through drills. The coaches would yell at him for his lack of focus, not realizing his head was in Pass Christian, Mississippi.

Ellis found comfort in his memories of his hometown, simply called "Pass" by locals. He recalled a place where preachers had southern drawls; where you could buy fresh shrimp at the local gas station; where kids learned to fish around the same age they learned to read. But Ellis had one memory most Pass residents didn't share: playing football in his front yard with Brett Favre. The famous quarterback is a native of nearby Kiln, Mississippi, and a friend of Ellis' father, so as Ellis puts it, "Brett Favre would come over and hang out." Sometimes, Favre would offer the Ellis kids $100 if they could catch a pass, throwing the ball into the Mississippi clouds. Other times, Favre tossed passes directly to Ellis, some of them so hard that it nearly knocked the wind out of the adoring teenager.

Sometimes Favre spent Mardi Gras in John Ellis' office, which was right on the main road in town. One year, during the festival, Ellis' younger brother Josh, then six years old, wore an inflatable football helmet. Unfortunately for him, it was a Dallas Cowboys helmet. Favre and fellow Packer Mark Chmura snatched it off Josh's head and stomped on it, destroying the rival team's headpiece. Frightened and confused, Josh couldn't stop crying, while his older brother couldn't stop laughing. Over time, Ellis was given numerous items autographed by his hero. But Katrina's waters flushed all of them away.

Before the meeting, Ellis had sat in the Dallas Doubletree business center alone, incessantly clicking through news websites. The phone conversations with his mother had been vague, and he worried she was keeping the extent of the damage to their home from him; he could hear it in her voice. The television news had shown passing images of Mississippi's Gulf Coast, and though Katrina was being billed as the "New Orleans' hurricane," he knew there was extensive damage near his hometown.

Ellis zoomed in on satellite images until he found Pass. His heart dropped as he examined the picture on the screen. He called his mom, who was staying at a hunting camp in the Mississippi Delta, and demanded she tell him the truth. She had been trying to spare her son from any more pain, especially considering how homesick he'd been, and especially because she wasn't there in person to hug him. But she knew the time to tell him had come.

Their home, she told him, was flattened. So was his older brother's home. His older sister's home was still standing, but the furniture and other valuables had floated out. And his father's office, right on the beach, where Brett Favre had spent

Mardi Gras with the Ellis family, was now nothing but an empty slab.

Despite news of the devastation, Ellis sat in the meeting, hoping, along with the other players, that their coach was right; that this fog would lift. These players understood Scelfo's dedication, and they understood their dedication to each other. Many members of the team knew the coming weeks would define them as a team more than any football game ever could. But there were 87 players, all of them with different perspectives, and not everyone felt the same way about what needed to happen next. Backup quarterback Chris Dawson said, "I noticed the two extremes. There were some people I thought who handled it really well with a lot of class and perspective, and a lot of people who acted like babies."

Some players wanted to go home—or to where home once was. Others wanted to go home and retrieve valuables. Some were just stir-crazy. There were players like Ellis, who, being a freshman, didn't know his teammates very well and wanted more than anything to be with his family. And then there were players like junior receiver Preston Brown, who'd grown up far from Katrina's devastation but was no less familiar with tough situations. Brown had been raised in the projects of Camden, New Jersey. He was one of five siblings, never knowing his father. He'd lived in 10 homes by the time he'd turned 18, many of them belonging to his mother's friends. He'd almost died in a house fire when he was just six years old. When he was nine, he ran to his grandmother's house to call 911 after finding his mother, a drug addict, sprawled on the floor, vomit trailing from her mouth after an overdose.

Brown spent his early years surrounded by drug use. At school, he got in fights and earned poor grades. He stole from stores, saw people robbed, and was himself robbed. He saw people get shot and had had a gun pulled on him. Around age 10, he started standing on street corner at 2 a.m. hustling addicts; he took bars of soap, cut them up, and sold "beat bags," which resembled crack, on street corners. Other times, he served as a lookout for neighborhood drug dealers. Brown, having seen firsthand the harm drugs caused his mother and his aunts, knew using drugs wasn't good. But he honestly felt *selling* drugs was a lifestyle he should be a part of, because it was all he knew.

When Brown was 12, the opportunity to escape life in Camden came into his life, disguised as a drug dealer. The guy saw something in Brown, something underneath the layers of naughtiness; the lookout boy had some charisma. For some reason, this drug dealer decided Brown needed structure. And he knew of a football league in the suburbs. The league had stopped allowing kids from the Camden area to play because there had been problems with fighting. But the drug dealer's grandmother lived in the area. He gave Brown the address to use during registration, as well as the $100 fee. But just prior to the sign-up date, Brown was mugged and the money was stolen. He figured it was one of his mother's friends who'd stolen the money to buy drugs. Learning this, the drug dealer decided to escort Brown to his first practice. He gave him another $100.

It was the first time in his life that Brown played organized football, and it became his salvation. Brown rode his bike 35 minutes each way just to get to the field. But nothing could stand in the way of his new pastime; he couldn't pedal fast enough.

By his senior year at Woodrow Wilson High, Preston Brown was a football sensation, blessed with long legs and a searing desire. He stood 6-foot-4, towering over even the tall corner-backs. He was considered one of the most athletic players in New Jersey. Each catch, each broken tackle, was a step closer towards the city limits. Touchdowns were going to get him out of town, out of America's shadows; the kid from the projects was working towards going to college for free.

Brown's mother was in jail during his senior season. She'd been the loudest parent in the stands the year before, so her absence the following season was conspicuous. People would ask the star receiver where his mom was. He would say she had to work, the lie painfully coming off his lips. In a game near Thanksgiving, where senior parents would put on their sons' oversized jerseys and escort them ceremoniously onto the field, Brown walked onto the field with his brother.

But it was during that parentless season that Brown connected with a father figure. As Scelfo's Tulane staff recruited Brown, the unlikely duo began to bond. The only thing Brown and Coach Scelfo had in common was that they both said "y'all." Brown was quintessentially urban, while Scelfo was unapologetically rural. Brown was tall and muscular; Scelfo, short and stocky. But Scelfo knew what it was like to try to play football without parents around. Brown's tough, suave demeanor didn't fool Scelfo; he recognized the lonely kid with a fragile heart. And Brown knew that Scelfo knew.

Coach Scelfo told Brown that, as a player at Tulane, he would be part of a family. For a kid like Preston Brown, those words had resonance. When Brown showed up in New Orleans that fall for an official recruiting visit, Scelfo told the young man that he loved him. "You don't know it now," the coach told the player, "but you'll know it in the future." Brown watched Tulane win the Hawaii Bowl that winter, and he knew that school was where he was supposed to be. He called Scelfo and committed to Tulane.

Brown struggled in his first few seasons, not seeing much playing time. He came close to transferring to Iowa, a school that had promised more time with the ball. But in the end, he stayed with Tulane because his teammates—and his coach—were his family. What did change was his determination to be a starter: "I just put it in my mind—I will never watch other people play again," Brown said. "People were going to come watch me play. . . . I had to work harder to put myself in a position where I couldn't be denied."

That summer, he had stayed in New Orleans and worked at a beer packaging company. In the afternoons after work, he would head to Tulane's campus to lift weights. Then, he would either run long distances or work on receiving drills. He would get home as the sun was going down and would rise before daybreak to be back at work by five the next morning. Day after day, he followed this meticulous routine to make sure he was the best receiver on campus. And it worked. He ended August training camp as Tulane's No. 1 target.

o o o

In that Sunday team meeting in the Dallas Doubletree conference room, Brown slouched in his chair, listening to his teammates bicker like children.

Players whose homes hadn't even hit by Katrina were whining about going home to retrieve personal items. Others, like Jordan Ellis, were homesick and wanted to return home to help their families cope with the storm's aftermath. Some players suggested that the team quit the 2005 season. The Tulane football team, at this moment, at this team meeting, was about to crack.

Brown couldn't believe what he was hearing. His strong family had deteriorated into an unsure and unstable group of guys, barely still a team. As someone whose home was thousands of miles from Louisiana but equally damaged, he decided he needed to say something. He stood up in front of the men and began to speak.

He talked about the troubles in his family, his mother's constant battle with drugs. He told them how football had been his salvation, even if it had come into his life through the efforts of a drug dealer. He told them about how Coach Scelfo had turned into the father he'd never known. And then, his voice cracking, he said: "I'm thousands of miles from my home. I see y'all every single day. Blood, sweat, tears, every day with y'all. This is my family right here. For y'all to be talking all this selfish talk—you want to go home, check on your apartment—we're supposed to be a family here, working on one common goal. But there's a whole bunch of individual ideas that are very segregated. You cannot progress as a unit if the individuals don't meet in the middle." Brown then had to stop speaking. He began crying uncontrollably. So did Anthony Cannon, a senior linebacker and Brown's close friend.

Brown hadn't lost anything material in the storm. But he would lose what mattered to him most if his teammates decided to quit. His admission—*I need this team; it's all I have*—made the rest of the players realize the importance of being, and remaining, a team. Before that meeting, the Tulane players could have very well elected to quit the season. But after that meeting, quitting wasn't an option. They were a family, and that was all they needed to know to keep going.

CHAPTER 8

Arrivals

The meeting where Preston Brown helped to convince his teammates to continue with the season had brought some much-needed clarity; they'd decided they were going to play, and that they were going to do it for each other. The team also understood and embraced the fact that they were not just representing a school. They would represent the entire city of New Orleans this season. They would be seen as a microcosm of post-Katrina society, uniting in the face of adversity. Never had a team with so little have so much to play for.

Heading into the second weekend at the Dallas Doubletree, those who had lost their homes had at least come to grips with that reality. And no player had lost a family member to the storm. Some of the players wanted time away from the hotel. After all, when they lived back in New Orleans, players weren't together every waking minute. But since the storm, they'd been seeing each other day in and day out. As Anthony Cannon put it, "Too much testosterone in one room is a bad equation."

Scelfo knew he couldn't let the team disperse. Brown's speech had inspired them to stay, and there was now a structure, albeit fragile. Scelfo solved the problem by making the weekend of Friday, September 9, "Family Weekend" at the hotel. Players wouldn't practice, and were encouraged to invite their families to Dallas.

From the moment Scelfo had entered the Dallas Doubletree, he'd been in constant motion, scampering through the lobby like one of his running backs in a seam. Rest was irrelevant. Scelfo didn't know anything about his home. He had heard some rumors about fires and looting in his neighborhood, which was called English Turn, but he didn't have time to care. The only thing that had slowed him down were the puppy-dog eyes of his 11-year-old son, Joseph. One afternoon during those first few days in the hotel, his son had wanted to play pool, so the coach made his way to the hotel's poolroom. Scelfo grabbed a stick, leaned against the table, and smacked the cue ball— which rolled a good eight inches to the right of the racked triangle of balls.

"At least you know I'm not hanging out in bars," he deadpanned.

He finally hit the triangle on his third try.

"I'm going on one goal right now," the delirious but determined Scelfo said between shots. "As we do in athletics, you ask any coach in America, from high school to the NFL, they want to be champions. Any coach—we want to win the Super Bowl, we want to win the conference, we want to win the district. That's not my individual goal. My team's goal is that they want to be champions. My goal, as the leader of the whole thing, I want to be able to say when that final horn sounds, 'We perse-vered.' When we do that, everybody in the city of New Orleans and everybody who was affected by this, whether they lived there or not, if we affect one person by giving them hope to per-severe, I'm the first one on the train to heaven."

With his mind somewhere in New Orleans, Scelfo set up a pool shot, took a deep breath, and pocketed the ball. Except the ball was one of Joseph's. The son laughed uproariously, and the father smiled. Joseph finally sank the 8-ball. Scelfo congratulat-ed his son and the pair made their way back into the lobby, back into uncertainty.

Scelfo's continuous struggle was, simply, creating normalcy amid abnormal circumstances, all the while abiding by the NCAA's rules—rules that had never been put up against a situ-ation like the one in which they found themselves. Dickson, the athletic director, had spoken to Scelfo and told him to watch what they were doing. Although Scelfo was in survival mode, Dickson reminded him that his actions, no matter how neces-sary they might seem, must not jeopardize the program. Scelfo felt insulted—he'd been trying to save the program. Frustrated, Scelfo finally asked Dennis Polian, the director of football oper-ations, to get a hold of Britton Banowsky, the commissioner of Conference USA.

Banowsky had fought diligently for Tulane to remain in his conference during the 2003 athletic review. Like Dickson and Scelfo, Banowsky understood the importance of athletics at Tulane remaining at the Division I-A level. Moreover, Tulane did it the right way: Scelfo's 75-percent graduation rate over the past four years was one of the nation's better graduation rates. Tulane student-athletes were constantly winning academic awards. And with football players across America stereotyped as unruly, Scelfo had never seen a player arrested in all his years as head coach.

Commissioner Banowsky lauded Tulane as a beacon in his conference, and now he was doing all he could to help the Green Wave in its most trying time. He'd helped coordinate the football team's move to Dallas, where Conference USA has its home. He'd also been part of the search to find Tulane football a new home for the season. They'd decided on Ruston, Louisiana, where Tulane athletes would "carry the torch, be the face, and represent the name" of the resilient university. And although it was a relief to know where they would next land, Scelfo was looking for raw, direct results. His players were suffering, and he felt the conference wasn't doing enough to help them.

On Wednesday, September 7, Banowsky met Scelfo in the Doubletree lobby. The coach looked weathered, a full cup of coffee in his hands. The two went for a drive in Banowsky's BMW, and Scelfo soon began to unleash his anger on the commissioner. Scelfo said it wasn't fair to make the football team "carry the torch" when it had nothing to light the fire. He felt that all the hard work by administrators in the days after Katrina helped with logistics and the sustainability of the athletic programs, but the individual football player was being overlooked. Although he had some good points, the coach found it difficult to control his anger. He used a lot of profanity, and eventually screamed for Banowsky to stop the car.

Scelfo stood on the side of the road, fuming. Then he launched his cup of coffee at the car as Banowsky sat patiently inside. In time, the coach calmed down. Banowsky invited him to his home, where they discussed the issues more serenely. But

Scelfo was unwavering in his belief that something more substantial needed to be done.

That night, Dickson called Scelfo's room. The athletic director was more than a little displeased by Scelfo's aggressive attitude. Scelfo erupted. With his wife Nancy by his side, Scelfo screamed at his boss for 20 minutes. He ended the conversation by hanging up on him. It was clear that Scelfo had reached the breaking point.

A few hours later, Dickson's wife, Brenda, came to the door. She said she had a message for Scelfo to call Dr. Scott Cowen. Cowen was the booming, dynamic president of Tulane. A dedicated educator, Cowen had been caught in the crossfire during the 2003 athletic review. He loved sports. He would sometimes show up to big Tulane games with his face painted green. He played college football himself and understood the value of a school's football program. But he also knew the cold facts. He was the president of an entire university. One of his departments was losing a lot of money, so he did a review to see how they could fix the problem. The department just happened to be athletics. And one of the possible fixes was dropping athletics to Division III.

But what transpired became ugly: Cowen became the villain in the eyes of the athletic department and Green Wave fans. They saw him simply as the one who was going to cut sports. It was a trying time for Cowen, who looked out his office window in June of 2003, the day before the Tulane Board voted to keep athletics, and saw some overzealous fan hanging his likeness in effigy.

But after the Tulane Board voted to keep athletics in Division I-A, Cowen's spot in the public eye made an about-face. Though his passion for sports hadn't changed, fans started looking to Cowen as the champion of the little guy. Cowen led a national crusade to spread the word about the inequities in college sports: how the Bowl Championship Series, which gives millions of dollars to teams only in BCS conferences, created a class system. He used Tulane as the ideal example. The system, the way it is, almost led to the downfall of a program that did things the right way. Some of the same fans who had cursed Cowen's name in June of 2003 later felt he should be the next president of the NCAA.

And so, in September of 2005, here was Cowen, on the phone with the football coach who stood by his team in 2003, and would again in 2005. Cowen had spent the first days riding a boat around his campus. His school was in shambles, and his football coach was disobeying orders when structure was imperative. Cowen was pleasant and understanding toward his coach, but he reaffirmed his stance that Dickson was in charge of the department of athletics, and Dickson knew how best to run the program, post-Katrina.

The dogged Coach Scelfo, who'd also been working to heal the multimillion-dollar college football program, soon admitted he'd "hit a wall." He wasn't sleeping. He was constantly guzzling coffee and working out logistics. Could it be possible that he cared too much?

Late one night during family weekend, Patti Terranova, Bubba's mom, was wandering the lobby. She spotted Chris and Nancy Scelfo sitting in the restaurant. It was closed.

Patti knew Coach Scelfo as the man who helped console her son after his fight at practice, as the one trying to keep the team together. She asked him how he was doing, expecting a standard, "I'm OK." Instead she got the truth.

"Things aren't really OK," he said. Scelfo told Patti he was afraid for the program, afraid his staff wouldn't be paid, afraid he couldn't do enough for his players, afraid that he couldn't get them through the season. But through his fear, Patti saw a genuine love. The emotions were on his weary face. She'd felt the same mixture herself just days earlier as she drove out of Slidell, with much of her life—and Bubba's—packed in the trunk of her Saturn. She'd ended up in a campground near Arcadia, Louisiana, where she stayed for the next week, tinkering with a little television, trying to catch a signal to get some news about Katrina. Eventually, she received a text message from her daughter. *Mom, it's really bad. Don't come home.*

On September 9, when Patti had finally united with her son during family weekend at the Dallas Doubletree, she hugged him with a linebacker's tackle. Everything is OK when Patti is with Bubba, when he cracks his corny jokes, when he flashes his schoolboy grin, when he listens with his heart. Her love for her son was just as visible on her face as Scelfo's was on his. She knew he would do anything for his team.

On Saturday, September 10, while the players spent time at the hotel with their families, a sleepless Coach Scelfo and his staff flew to Ruston to visit the facilities. Then on Monday he was going to travel with the team on the bus to Ruston, where the players would register for classes and tour the campus. The morning of the day they were supposed to leave for Ruston, Dickson called Scelfo and said Dr. Cowen was flying in for a meeting that would happen later that day.

When the Tulane president walked in the room, Scelfo could tell he was worn out. Cowen, like Scelfo, had dedicated the past weeks to saving the school. And Cowen's task of revitalizing a major university was, after all, unprecedented. Cowen sat at the head of the table, with Scelfo to his left and Dickson to his right. Cowen told Scelfo that he appreciated his commitment to his team, but felt the coach needed to remain in Dallas for a while, perhaps get some professional help and, quite simply, get some rest. This, of course, might mean Scelfo would miss the first game of the season, the September 17 game against Mississippi State.

"Doc," Scelfo said, "The only thing I can tell you is this: I'm going to Ruston, Louisiana, tonight. I'm either going as a father and a husband, or I'm going as your head football coach."

Cowen still felt that Scelfo needed rest, away from the team. He argued it would be for the good of the team.

"Well Doc," Scelfo said, "you have to do what you have to do, and I feel like I have to do what I have to do, and I'll guaran-dang-tee you this: I don't need this job. I want this job, because there's not another person around here who can lead this team through the season. If you don't believe that, then I probably just need to go on to Ruston as a father and a husband. But I'm going to Ruston. Those players need me."

Though worried about the coach's well being, and frustrated by the coach's steadfast determination, Cowen decided to remove himself from this football situation. He had a university to save. He charged Dickson with the task of finding common ground with Scelfo, and with making sure Scelfo was ready to coach.

That afternoon, Scelfo and Dickson sat down together. Scelfo told Dickson he needed a greater sense of urgency from everyone involved in Tulane football. He felt like he was doing the job of five men. He handled countless details involving the football team. He told Dickson he needed a support staff of equipment managers, a trainer, and a sports information director. After the storm, Tulane lost the people who filled those roles, which meant Dickson had to be resourceful with his remaining employees. He asked Dickson for his and Cowen's support, and he asked them to have faith in him.

At the end of their conversation, the two shook hands. It was a peaceful end to a long and difficult weekend. And that night, Scelfo went to Ruston—a father, a husband, and a coach.

○ ○ ○

For Patti Terranova, however, the family weekend had gone by too quickly. By that Monday, all of the other parents had already left, but Patti couldn't make herself go, making excuses to delay her departure. Soon the players began loading the busses. Patti was forced to say goodbye to Bubba. She drove her Saturn behind the Tulane busses for 15 minutes, tears falling down her face. Finally, they reached the highway entrances. Bubba headed to Ruston; Patti headed to New Orleans.

Lost in her depression, Patti drove into the darkness. Her plan was to visit what was left of her home and piece things together. Approaching midnight, she exited Interstate 10 onto Highway 11. The only visible lights came from her headlights. She crawled down the street, one eye on the road, the other on the surrounding devastation. Buildings had collapsed. Brick walls had been knocked down. Cars were flipped upside down on the side of roads. So were boats. Trees, if standing at all, were barren.

She stayed at her daughter's apartment that night, which was on a second floor and had survived the storm. But Patti couldn't sleep; she kept worrying what the area would look like once the sun came up.

On Tuesday morning, September 13, while her son was miles away on a new campus, Patti got out of bed at 5:30 a.m. and drove to her home, which had been besieged with five feet of floodwater. Her daughter had been there earlier in the month. She and a friend had removed the larger items from the home. So there on Patti's front lawn sat her sofa, television, refrigerator, and bed, all the pieces moldy and useless.

She opened her front door slowly, afraid of what she might see. The smell hit Patti right in the face, a vicious, brutal odor of mold. Inside, countertops had buckled, caked with soot and mud. The bathtub was filled with brown dirty water; Patti feared snakes swimming inside. Books, clothing, framed photos of Bubba—all her possessions were littered on the floor. She started frantically grabbing items off the ground, checking to see if they were salvageable. Overwhelmed, she suddenly paused.

"Poof, it was all gone," she said. "In an instant."

But she still had one thing, one symbol of normalcy. Her son was out of harm's way, safe on a college campus, preparing for a football game. In four days, her son would be back on the field, and she would be there, cheering in the stands, ready to witness the beginning of his team's extraordinary season.

CHAPTER 9

Ruston

*W*ithin the 48 hours following Hurricane Katrina, Tech athletic director Jim Oakes had contacted Conference USA's offices to offer his university to Tulane. What Tech was doing was unprecedented. Although the school had a quaint athletic department that cherished what facilities they had, they'd decided to give any excess facility space to the Tulane football team. Tech embraced the Green Wave, sharing not just their athletic facilities, but their dorms and classrooms as well.

Jim King, Tech's vice president for student affairs, orchestrated the unenviable task of enrolling 87 students into Tech classes—just a week before classes began. Tech officials pieced together class schedules, matching majors and year in school. They found books and school supplies. They provided meal plans for the players and staff to eat on campus. They held a thorough orientation. They did all of this while they also took care of the 11,000 students already enrolled.

The Tech community rallied around their new neighbors. Donations came from James Davison, a multimillionaire and resident of Ruston who'd arranged for housing for the coaches; sororities made weekly goodie bags for the players; school officials found housing for the coaches and their families, if they hadn't evacuated elsewhere; Karl Malone, the retired NBA legend and former Tech star, gave a speech to the Green Wave; and before Tulane arrived, the Tech football team had carried mattress after mattress up the sweltering dorm stairs to prepare the rooms for their arrival.

The team would be living in Caruthers Hall, a dilapidated dormitory on the Louisiana Tech University campus that had been scheduled to be torn down. But after Hurricane Katrina, when an exodus of New Orleans residents headed north toward Ruston, Tech figured any shelter was better than none, so it reopened the doors of the dorm. The hurricane evacuees from Tulane moved in on September 12.

To say that Ruston is a small town would be an understatement. Driving west on Interstate 20, the first symbol of Ruston is a big blue sign at Exit 86, which reads "ATTRACTIONS"—but none are listed. In Ruston, a Chili's restaurant constitutes the finest dining around. Every morning, the local radio station features the "Daily Farm Report." Deer corn is available at most gas stations. When residents learn that a local horse is pregnant, it becomes big news. The team, which was used to city life, would have to find a way to make Ruston feel like home.

In New Orleans, Tulane football operations occupied dozens of offices, state-of-the-art locker rooms, weight rooms, and meeting rooms. There were elliptical machines and chipper secretaries and trophy cases and elaborate video projectors fit for a Cineplex. Even graduate assistants had their own offices. Coach Scelfo's office had a terrace, overlooking the sunny practice field. That kind of comfort was not going to be the case in Ruston, where two athletic programs would have to share one campus. The Tulane locker room, for instance, didn't have lockers. Instead, dozens of chairs were set up in a vacant room, a sheet of paper with a uniform number taped above each chair, an equipment bag placed in front. The team shared the weight room with Louisiana Tech athletes, often waiting patiently to sneak in a lift. Player meeting rooms were in one big room. The night before the first practice in their new home, the coaches stayed up past midnight to construct makeshift walls made of Styrofoam, dividing the space into separate meeting rooms. In each created area, coaches placed chairs and a dry erase board. Sheets of paper indicating position—"DBs" or "QBs" or "WRs"—were slapped near the entrance of each area.

In meetings, positional coaches tried to capture intimacy with their players, maximizing precious meeting time to dissect the opposition. Alas, these sessions were often muddled and distracting; the thin walls were essentially useless, and coaches' voices collided. In position meetings, players caught themselves listening to other coaches instead of their own.

At practices back home, Tulane normally had six employees handling medical duties. Because Tulane's athletic teams dispersed to five different universities that semester, only trainer Justin LeDuc and his assistant, Miesty Woodburn, went to Louisiana Tech, taping ankles until their own wrists needed to be taped. Also, on their own campus, the Green Wave had six people who dealt with equipment and manager duties, be it student volunteers, interns, or full-time staff members. In Ruston, they had only equipment manager John Mendow and his assistant, Chico Rodriguez.

Mendow, a hefty Louisianan with a penchant for chewing tobacco, was an underpaid, overworked company man. But in Ruston, the equipment manager didn't have any equipment. When the team frantically packed the busses that Sunday before the storm, it packed for the week—not for the entire 2005 season. Tulane did have practice essentials: helmets, shoulder pads, soft pads, pants, and practice cleats. They had road uniforms, which were all they needed considering they wouldn't have a game in New Orleans. But they lacked a few essential pieces; they didn't have, among other things, game helmets.

Mendow woke each morning with the sun, popped some Skoal in his mouth, and began working the phones, seeking donations of "helmet hardware, strings, socks, gloves, backup shoes, footballs—anything and everything." He would often have a phone in one hand and a tool in the other as he repaired some recently broken piece of equipment. He worked until sundown every day, only to start the next with the phone back at his ear.

As mid-September approached, Tulane still didn't know where it would play its home games. Shreveport, Louisiana, offered its stadium for the entire season, but school officials thought it might be a better idea to play in different cities around the state because fans had been scattered everywhere. The only thing certain was that the first game, on September 17 against Mississippi State, would be an hour down the road from Ruston, at Shreveport's Independence Stadium.

In Starkville, Mississippi, the Mississippi State Bulldogs prepared for Tulane in their brand new, 46,000-square foot athletic center. There was a plush locker room with spacious lockers, meeting rooms, and a theater with stadium seating. There was a players' lounge with a pool table and leather couches, a training room with a hydrotherapy pool, and a weight room with $350,000 worth of equipment.

After Tulane practices, the players lumbered back toward Caruthers Hall, where they were often greeted by a broken elevator. And so they climbed the stairs to their rooms, some as high as the eighth floor. Their dorm rooms were always hot, no matter how much they fiddled with the shoddy air conditioner. The mattresses felt full of bricks. The faucets in some rooms dripped sporadically and infuriatingly. They hadn't lived there very long, but it was already clear to the Tulane players why the dorm had originally been condemned.

The Tulane players were not the only ones calling Caruthers home. The dorm's lower floors housed other hurricane victims. Men in T-shirts sat around tables in the lounges, playing endless card games. Little girls with braids in their hair rode toy scooters around the front pavement. Desperate parents stood around with their cell phones to their ears, waiting to get through to a human at FEMA. Elderly ladies with stories to tell sat in the cafeteria or laundry room and waited for listeners.

The Turner family were also Caruthers residents. The Turners—Catherine, her husband Ricky, and daughters Ricketa and Lauren—lost their home and four vehicles to the storm. Their neighborhood became a wasteland, and despite the Army tents that sprouted up around town, the Turners found themselves homeless. The Turners decided to come to Ruston, where Lauren, 21, could attend Tech. They were just driving down the street when they saw people moving into Caruthers. By nightfall, they had a temporary home. The girls enrolled in classes—

Ricketa went to Ruston High—and Ricky was back and forth from Phoenix, Louisiana, to Ruston for work.

Catherine spent her days at the dorm, assisting with tutoring and day care. Other days, she just sat out front, took deep breaths, and swapped stories. She was a therapist without a couch. She embraced her role as a surrogate mother to the evacuees in Caruthers Hall, creating smiles even when she had trouble smiling herself. "I'm not as strong as they think I am," she said.

Catherine compared what her family was going through to a nightmare, one of those scary, chilling nightmares that you wake up from, squeeze your pillow, and thank the Lord that it was just a bad dream. "Well," she said, "I'm still waiting to wake up."

Some of the football players kept their distance from the occupants of floors 1-4; there was no way to know who they were, and they weren't part of their team. But a funny thing happened in the laundry room. The Tulane players, some just months removed from their parents' homes, would walk in nervously with a basket of whites and a stack of quarters. They would load the washer to the brim, while residents like the Turners would lock eyes and smile. The non-Tulane residents with a bit more laundry experience, seeing the players' mistakes, would help them with their laundry. While the dryer tumbled, they talked about life, Katrina, Ruston, and uncertainty. It was in the laundry room where the players realized everyone in Caruthers was in the same situation, facing the same problems; they were all hurricane evacuees. The only difference was that some of them had plans on Saturdays.

Among the weathered faces of evacuees was a 13-year-old boy named Cordell. Like Tulane's Preston Brown, Cordell was born in a rough area: the Calliope projects in the Third Ward of New Orleans, known for its violence after dark. Cordell's mother eventually moved her son to the Gentilly neighborhood of New Orleans. But Hurricane Katrina had destroyed Gentilly, which forced Cordell to seek shelter in Ruston.

Cordell could often be found roaming aimlessly around the dormitory. He was scared and angry. He couldn't harness his emotions, so he rebelled at school, getting into fights, and he soon found himself suspended. At Caruthers Hall, he would follow the football players, and he started to look up to them. He thought, these guys have it all—large muscles, exceptional talent, and most importantly, college scholarships. It never really occurred to Cordell that some of the players had once been like him.

But it had occurred to Brandon Spincer. The linebacker would spot Cordell in the hallways, peeking around corners. One day in September, the two New Orleans natives started talking about home, and it turned out that Cordell used to play football at Shakespeare Park, where Spincer had played a decade earlier. Eventually Cordell worked up enough courage to ask Spincer if he could come with him to one of his linebackers meetings. Spincer obliged, and Cordell sat in, listening intently to indecipherable football jargon. After the meeting, he followed Spincer to practice and watched in awe from the sideline. After practice, the soft-spoken Cordell thanked Spincer.

The next day, like a puppy, Cordell was there again, following Spincer to his meeting and practice. Then in the weight room, Cordell watched the chiseled Spincer do his lifts; then Spincer taught Cordell how to do arm curls. The two shared a sandwich and a Gatorade before another meeting. Again, Cordell lost himself in football talk until he began to doze off.

The players had a good laugh at coach Garret Chachere's expense—he'd bored the kid to sleep.

Cordell started popping into Spincer's life off the field, at Caruthers, asking him questions and, before he could answer them, peppering him with more. One day, Spincer asked Cordell about his father. Cordell suddenly became angry: "I don't know where that punk at." Cordell wouldn't admit it, but living without a father gnawed at his stomach. He'd channeled his emotions into curse words and bad behavior. Spincer had seen this happen in many of his fatherless classmates growing up in New Orleans; he always knew he was lucky to have both parents. In his neighborhood, it would have been easy to join a gang or hide in alcohol; some of his friends had done just that. Spincer knew he had to help Cordell, and he did everything he could to teach Cordell the lessons he'd never been taught.

○ ○ ○

It was finally game week. For the first time since the storm had crawled north, the Tulane Green Wave felt the happiness that comes with a routine. There was the Monday press conference; the game preparation meetings; the calls from family about tickets. Tulane's football team, 20 days after Hurricane Katrina, was going to play a game. And it had become a major event. For the first time ever, America Online would broadcast a game live on the Internet. And there would also be a telethon during the game with celebrities asking viewers to donate to hurricane victims.

At the press conference, wearing the same long-sleeved gray shirt he wore for much of the fall, Scelfo said: "This isn't about winning and losing. This is about perseverance. If we can give one person hope back in our Tulane community and our city of New Orleans, then I feel like we will have accomplished our goals."

During Thursday's practice, right after special teams drills, Spincer stood on the sun-splashed field next to Cordell. Coach Scelfo knew what an effect his own protégé, Spincer, had made on his young protégé. So Scelfo invited Cordell to join the team at the first game.

Tulane's journey had begun on a bus to Jackson, then continued on another to Dallas and another to Ruston. And on September 17, 2005, they would load another bus to Shreveport for their historic season opener.

CHAPTER 10

Game Day

On Saturday morning in Ruston, the only noise Coach Scelfo made during breakfast came from his silverware. Normally at meals, his enthusiastic son, Joseph, peppered him with questions about football. On a game day, however, the Scelfos knew it was one of the 11 days in the year where questions waited until Sunday.

Coach Scelfo was confident. He'd injected confidence into his players every day at practice. He knew he had motivated his players through the most difficult month of their lives. He saw their resilience in the way they practiced and in the way they carried themselves around Tech's campus. And he knew he had a talented football team on paper. But how would they respond in their first game after Katrina? He picked at his food; his mind transported an hour down the road, to Shreveport.

○ ○ ○

In the locker room at Independence Stadium, Cordell helped Spincer put on his shoulder pads, and then accompanied the linebacker onto the field for pregame warm-ups. Cordell's eyes remained wide as he stood on the glistening field, surrounded by the stadium seats, which were just starting to fill. The team returned to the locker room for Coach Scelfo's rousing speech—"Not for thyself, but for others."

The players then lined up in the dark tunnel, bouncing up and down, waiting to erupt onto the field. Cordell caught Spincer's eyes through his facemask. "Y'all better go and win this game," he said.

"I'm going to win this game for you," Spincer told him.

○ ○ ○

Sundown brought with it a clear Louisiana evening, a welcome calm after the storm. Thousands of Tulane fans, mired in post-hurricane depression, united that night in Shreveport. There were the Ballard brothers, proud alums and owners of a chicken wing chain in New Orleans, who'd postponed a meeting with an insurance adjuster to attend the first game. There were Kim and John Ellis, who hadn't seen their son, the freshman Jordan, since he'd left Pass Christian for college. And there was Patti Terranova, who'd thought of the game as her only solace as she dealt with the destruction of her home that week.

Patti was wearing her son's jersey, something she'd worn every autumn Saturday up to that point. Receiver Bubba Terranova had bought it for her years earlier. It was an authentic jersey with TERRANOVA 17 stitched on the back. The jersey was heavy and hot, and it hung low; give her a belt and some stockings, and she had a one-piece dress. But she wore it to every game, be it in New Orleans, Houston, or Honolulu. In four years, she'd never missed one. The jersey had been one of the first things she'd placed in her trunk when she was forced to abandon her home and evacuate.

So there she was at Shreveport's Independence Stadium, in her green jersey. Only 16,421 people were in attendance, but the people who made the journey that night had a burning desire to be there. "It was therapy," Patti said. "Oh my God, I needed that game so badly."

Bubba had been Patti's therapist once before, when she went though a divorce during Bubba's senior year. He was Patti's rock. When Patti had dropped Bubba off at his dorm for the first time, in August of 2002, she had cried the whole drive home even though he was only living 30 miles away. Every single weekend, she would drive into Orleans Parish to do her son's laundry.

When the Tulane players spilled onto the field, Patti began to squint, feverishly trying to spot No. 17. And when she did, "from that very second, I didn't see anything else. The whole world disappeared. All I saw was him. I could feel him."

On the field, in his gleaming white uniform, Bubba scanned the crowd. He spotted his mother and suddenly felt calm and safe. He also spotted other familiar faces: a player's dad, a classmate, an athletic booster. This was a football game, but it was bigger than football. From out on the field, Bubba could sense how much this game meant to the people in the stands. Just as Coach Scelfo had said throughout September, Terranova and his teammates were playing for a university and a city. They were representing resilience, inspiring those who felt handcuffed by the storm. They were playing for people like his mom.

On the other side of the Shreveport stands, thousands of fans wore maroon and dozens clanged cowbells. The MSU Bulldog fans are a proud bunch from a struggling state and a struggling football program. They're members of the mighty Southeastern Conference, which is annually regarded as college football's finest. MSU fans always show up clanging cowbells, be it at the coach's Monday night radio show or at a Saturday morning tailgate.

These fans were in a tricky situation this Saturday in Shreveport, because they knew what Tulane had been through, and was still going through. They saw Scelfo on the field wearing a long-sleeved athletic shirt and shorts because he didn't have time to shop for game-day attire. They had read the stories and seen the broadcasts about Tulane's makeshift conditions. They saw the sparse crowd on the other sideline, knowing many Green Wave fans who wanted to be there couldn't make the trip. But Mississippi State's football team was going to honor Tulane by playing as hard as it could. And the Bulldog fans understood the only thing they could do was clang their cowbells and root proudly and loudly. It would have been insulting to Tulane if they didn't take the game seriously.

Besides, this was game day. The Bulldogs didn't win too often. This was a chance to grab a victory, on the road, no less. They weren't going to let this opportunity slip. "Out there on the field," Spincer said, "there ain't no sympathy." After all, this was the Tulane team that beat the Bulldogs two seasons before in one of Coach Scelfo's most impressive victories. At the Superdome in 2003, the Green Wave made a 17-point fourth-quarter comeback, capped off by a game-winning 32-yard field goal by freshman kicker Barrett Pepper. It was Pepper's first collegiate field goal.

The next season, Mississippi State had a new coach, Sylvester Croom, the first African-American head coach in the history of the Southeastern Conference. His first game was against Tulane. The Green Wave showed up in Starkville for that game in 2004, and in Lester Ricard's first game at quarterback, Tulane struggled to find any offensive rhythm, losing 28-7. And now, a year later in Shreveport, Tulane and Mississippi State faced each other again in a football game that would be historic regardless of who won.

That night, the American flag was displayed at half-staff. Coach Scelfo pressed his right hand on his chest on a green Tulane logo as the national anthem played. No hurricane or emotional meltdown was going to keep him from coaching his team. From New Orleans to Jackson to Dallas to Ruston, Coach Scelfo had kept this team intact for *this* moment. The Tulane football team was going to play a game, and he was going to make sure its members played their hardest.

Tulane won the coin toss, and they elected to receive. Izzy Route collected the kickoff on the Tulane 1-yard line, and ran to the 18. But there was penalty against Tulane for a block in the back, and Tulane fittingly began its season with its back against the wall.

On the first play, Ricard handed the ball to running back Matt Forté for a 5-yard gain. On second down, Ricard faked a handoff to Forté and rolled right. Receiver Kenneth Guidroz was running down the right sideline, wide open, a wobbling corner-back trying to keep up. Just weeks before, Guidroz had thought his uncles had died in the hurricane. Now he was playing a foot-ball game, about to make a beleaguered team proud and a beleaguered fan base smile. But Ricard's pass sailed incomplete above Guidroz's head.

On third down, tight end Bobby Hoover dropped a 5-yard pass. Out trotted Chris Beckman, the All-Conference Tulane punter. Meanwhile, senior linebackers Spincer, Cannon, and Antonio Mason stood next to each other on the Tulane sideline, snarling. They were hungry not just for tackles, but also for glory. They made a bet about who would make the first tackle. Each linebacker, of course, bet on himself. Right before the first snap, Cannon quickly lifted his left foot, then his right, like a thoroughbred ready to explode out of the gate. And then he was off. Mississippi State quarterback Omarr Conner snapped the ball and Cannon catapulted toward running back Jerious Norwood. Avoiding a collision with Tulane's ferocious playmaker, Norwood cut to his right, but into the body of Tulane defensive end Billy Harrison for a measly 1-yard gain. On the next play, Norwood ran toward a crumbling offensive line and found himself smothered in white jerseys. Spincer, who was on the opposite side of the field, hopped to the fringe of the pile and jumped up and down.

On third-and-11, Conner received the ball in the shotgun formation and quickly looked to his left. There was Tulane safety Sean Lucas, Cannon's roommate and best friend, making a diagonal beeline toward the quarterback's blindside. Sensing the blitz, the flustered Conner glanced toward the center of the field, and then back at Lucas. Conner hastily flung the football while Lucas simultaneously pummeled him to the ground. The pass floated out of bounds near the cornerback Route, who began pumping his right fist while running off the field. Not one receiver had been even close.

Ricard's first pass of this possession hit linebacker Clarence McDougal right in the hands. The ball ricocheted onto the turf, just an incomplete pass on the stat sheet, but it could have been a turning point if intercepted. Ricard's next pass landed at the feet of a Mississippi State assistant coach. Scelfo quickly reviewed his quarterback's quartet of passes—overthrown, under thrown, nearly intercepted, nearly in the next state—and decided to call a draw play on third-and-10. Forté snatched the delayed hand-off and scurried for 10 yards and one inch, and Tulane, on its own 34-yard line, had its first first down. But it quickly became third down after two measly runs.

On third down, Ricard tiptoed to his right and spotted Preston Brown. The ball hit Brown in the hands, while three defenders converged. It was the first catch of Brown's college career. Guidroz, a receiver in a tight end's body, smashed the defender about to tackle Brown, and Brown ran for a 20-yard gain. Brown had already emerged as a team leader at the Dallas Doubletree. That September night in Shreveport, he emerged as a team star.

But three plays after Brown's first catch, the punter Beckman was back on the field.

The rest of the first quarter, and the second quarter too, became a square dance around midfield, a do-si-do of offensive futility. Round and round they went in the first half: six total punts by Mississippi State, seven by Tulane. Not a point was scored. Tulane's defense allowed just one first down the entire half.

The square dance continued into the third quarter, until the Bulldogs' Norwood suddenly slipped away. With 13:53 left in the third, Norwood shook the equilibrium of the scoreless football game from the Tulane 43-yard line. Tulane had loaded the defensive line with six players, and a seventh, Spincer, loomed just two yards behind. It seemed almost mathematically impossible for a Tulane player not to end up in the backfield. Sure enough, Alvin Johnson was back long before Conner handed the ball to Norwood. But Norwood slipped out of Johnson's grasp, and with the defensive line sucked into the pocket, Norwood ran down the field until Spincer dragged him down from behind, just eight yards from the end zone. Just three plays later, Conner tossed a pass to Norwood for the game's first touchdown. Then, seven minutes later, the Bulldogs doubled the score on another Conner touchdown pass.

The whispers from those watching in the stands became louder: Is Mississippi State that good, or is Tulane that bad? Has the hurricane taken its toll on Tulane? Once again, it was Preston Brown who grabbed his team by the facemask and yanked. On the first play of the next drive, Brown caught a tricky pass and then stutter-stepped past a safety, galloping for 23 yards. He slammed the football into the ground. Mississippi State was nervous; Ricard rediscovered the swagger he'd left on campus before the storm.

Three completed passes later, Ricard completed his master-stroke: a perfectly lofted pass into the back right corner of the end zone. Receiver Damarcus Davis, a Shreveport native, leapt to grab it. He caught the pass over his right shoulder as he sailed through mid-air, then landed in the end zone: touchdown, Tulane.

Erin Healan, a Tulane cheerleader, shrieked; she finally had a reason to cheer. Those first days after Katrina, the peppy Healan was stuck on her parents' couch in Georgia. She knew nothing about her Uptown apartment. She hadn't been able to locate her closest friends—her fellow cheerleaders—and all she knew was that they were scattered, but she didn't know where. When Healan learned that Tulane would play football that season, she knew she had to be at the games. At times in the past, cheerleading had seemed frivolous. But now, more than ever, she knew the Tulane players needed support.

Healan and her friends dedicated themselves to uniting the squad. Anjela Jenkins created a website for the cheerleaders to post their contact information. It also had driving directions to the games. The squad had 27 men and women entering the season. That night in Shreveport, five girls stood on the sideline. They didn't have any fancy cheers or back-bending stunts. They didn't even have pompoms, and they hadn't located their coach. They just screamed "Go Wave!" as loud and as often as they could. Just like the Tulane fans, the Tulane cheerleaders had reunited, wearing their classic green and white uniforms that they had planned to wear to Fan Day on August 28. After the insanity and uncertainty following the storm, the squad was doing something as normal as walking onto a field for a game. For Healan, normalcy was surreal. Shortly before kickoff, there had been a photo montage on the video screen of images from New Orleans. Healan, who had driven hours to cheer, had cried.

After Tulane's first touchdown, Mississippi State went three-and-out. But Tulane, trailing 14-7, punted the ball right back, and the cowbells clanged.

It was now the fourth quarter. People bit their fingernails; stomachs growled. Patti Terranova squirmed in her seat. On the field, Tulane's defensive line had been reduced to a quartet of matadors, whisking their bodies away from Norwood with ease. The running back bulldozed for 8 yards, followed by 9 and then 2, for another first down. The quarterback Conner mixed up his play calling with a pass, and almost threw an interception to Izzy Route, the scrappy cornerback/kick returner who hailed from the same high school as Cannon and Lucas. Conner temporarily redeemed himself with a completion on the next play, but after that, Route again terrorized the Bulldogs. This time, he sped into the backfield and knocked the ball-carrying Norwood off his feet for a 5-yard loss.

In a matter of plays, Tulane's defense went from insipid to inspired. And here came their reward. The play actually began favorably for the Bulldogs, a crisp Conner pass to Will Prosser at the Tulane 45. And that's where it ended for the Bulldogs, or at least a millisecond later when Prosser ran into a brick wall that was safety Darren Sapp. The result was a vicious, dizzying collision and a Bulldog fumble.

Lucas happened to be right there. He looked down at the lonely football. It was as if he paused, just for an instant, to capture the reality; this was too good to be true. Then, Lucas scooped up the ball and sprinted into the red zone, while Sapp and Prosser slowly rose from the mat.

Tulane had the ball on their opponent's 28. Six plays later, the Green Wave found itself in an undesirable third-and-10, and while kicker Jacob Hartgroves loosened up on the sideline, Coach Scelfo called the same draw play he did way back in the first quarter. It was again third-and-10, but the difference was the ball carrier. This time, it was Jovon Jackson, the wise, proud senior who shared the backfield with Forté. Here, on this draw play, Jackson was at his best, rumbling well past the first down marker and then into the end zone, an 18-yard score. There was 9:35 left to play and, at 14-14, it was anybody's ballgame.

Coach Scelfo gathered his team on the sideline. For weeks, he'd been giving them motivation and determination, and now, in a tie game, he did more of the same, telling them that they must win individual battles and remained poised.

Once back in the game, the Tulane defense forced a punt. The punted football floated in the sky, lathered in momentum.

When it landed, it slipped right out of Route's hands. "My heart dropped," Spincer said of the mistake. Mississippi State corralled the football on Tulane's 17-yard line and, with the momentum now tucked under his arm, Norwood shimmied into the end zone on the very next play. Just like that, the score was 21-14, Mississippi State.

The scoreboard game clock read 7:44; Tulane was now battling both time and the bulldogs. All night for Tulane, small mistakes kept getting in the way of offensive success. Occasionally, there was offensive harmony, but too often there were crucial lapses. On the first down of Tulane's most important drive, right tackle Derek Rogers turned his body left, while defensive end Willie Evans whisked past his right shoulder. Evans threw Ricard to the ground on the Tulane 11. The quarterback made up the yardage with an 8-yard pass to Brown on the following play, but Ricard followed that with an errant incompletion. With 6:43 left, it was fourth-and-long from their own 19.

Coach Scelfo learned his football from his father, but he learned cooking from his mother. She was a Cajun queen in the kitchen, often spicing up supper with some ingenious twist. There was just something irresistible about that creativity, that gambling, that element of surprise. And sometimes, Coach Scelfo spiced up his Saturdays the same way. He was the guy who had called for an onside kick on the opening play of the 2002 Hawaii Bowl; his team recovered the ball. Another time, he had called for a fake punt pass from his own red zone; the receiver was wide open, nothing but green in front of him, but he forgot to catch the ball before taking off.

From a strategic standpoint, a fake punt pass here against Mississippi State made some sense. Tulane was pinned pretty deep in its own territory. A good punt would push the Bulldogs back, but give them a lot of field to slowly conquer, milking the clock. A bad punt would give the Bulldogs good field position, and an opportunity to quickly put more points on the board. A fake punt pass would surely catch the Bulldogs by surprise, and the Tulane team could use another jolt. And honestly, Ricard seemed to be struggling to push the team up the field. So Scelfo decided to give punter Chris Beckman a shot. Beckman, an ex-high school quarterback who'd considered playing baseball for Mississippi State, prepared for the snap.

Brown darted down the left sideline and Beckman lofted a gorgeous ball to his teammate, while jaws dropped from Shreveport to Starkville. Brown corralled the pass for a 27-yard gain—Tulane's longest play of the night. The defender guarding Brown was flagged for pass interference, which meant that Tulane, who just seconds ago had its heels on its goal line, was now at midfield.

But that all changed when defensive end Evans once again blew past Rogers, and once again sacked Ricard. The quarterback completed second down to Guidroz and hit receiver Cary Koch for a screen pass on third. But the Bulldogs pounced on Koch as soon as he caught the ball, and he fell to the ground on the 49-yard-line, seven long yards from a first down. Beckman humbly returned to the field. This time, he punted, the ball landing at the Bulldogs 7-yard line.

Out trotted Norwood, the type of player who would show up on Saturdays in Gainesville, Florida or in Tuscaloosa, Alabama, just like the maroon-clad faithful would: with a chip on his shoulder pads. But that's the type of player a coach wants rushing the football because they cherish each yard. In his past six rushes against Tulane, Norwood averaged 6.2 yards, and now his Bulldogs were pinned against their end zone with 3:45 left.

He went for five yards on the first play and 13 more on the second. But two ill-fated plays brought Mississippi State to third-and-9 on its 26. The clock was suddenly the Bulldogs' enemy, too, as they had only 2:05 left in the game. If Mississippi State earned a first down here, the game would be over. On this third down, with every player clumping to his left, Conner went to his right. And what is normally a game of 11 men versus 11 men was reduced to a simple battle of one-on-one: Conner versus Spincer. The looming linebacker was the only Tulane player in the area close enough to make a play. And there was no way that Brandon Spincer, the fiercely proud senior from hurricane-ravaged New Orleans, was going to let this Bulldog get a first down.

Spincer wrapped up the slippery quarterback on the 30-yard-line, making a heroic play. Cordell, still watching his mentor from the sideline, cheered wildly. Mississippi State punted the ball one last time. Route, with visions of his fumble still floating in his helmet, caught the punt and picked up 15 yards, making it to the Green Wave 36. There was 1:17 left in the game.

Ricard threw an incomplete pass, and then fed Forté twice: an 11-yard run and a 1-yard run. It was second-and-9 on the Tulane 48. Coach Scelfo called timeout with 26 seconds left. Patti could barely watch. Bubba could only watch. The coaches had opted for other receivers, and Terranova was on the bench, a spectator during the final drive. He was normally stoic and agreeable; what Coach says, goes. But Terranova just stood there, brooding on the sideline, handcuffed. He began to seethe.

His mother was in the stands, and all they had left was family and football. All he wanted was a chance.

Ricard's deep pass to Davis fell incomplete. Now it was third down. Terranova continued to fume: he was the oldest receiver on the team; he had already made four catches that night; he knew he could make a play. This game was too important to lose. He could not let them lose it.

Ricard's deep pass to Guidroz fell incomplete. Fourth down. Terranova finally erupted. In a profanity-laced plea to receivers coach Darryl Mason, he screamed: "Put me in there!" Mason gave him a shot. "I heard it in his voice," Mason said. "And saw it in his eyes."

Fourteen seconds remained when Terranova hustled onto the field. It was fourth-and-9 from the 48. This was it. Ricard took the snap from the shotgun position, three receivers to his right, only Terranova to his left. Ricard briskly dropped back three steps and winged the ball toward Terranova. He caught it: first down, Tulane.

Coach Scelfo called timeout. There were eight fateful seconds left. Tulane had the ball on the Mississippi State 39-yard line. With the Green Wave down one touchdown, this would either be the last play of regulation or the last play of the game. Tulane needed a prayer, so they called for a Hail Mary. During the timeout, Coach Scelfo, his face drenched in perspiration, barked commands: Ricard would look to the right side of the end zone. The 6-foot-4 Brown was to set up at the goal line. Brian King was to dart for the back right corner of the end zone; if the ball was tipped back by the towering Brown, the freshman receiver would be behind Brown to catch it. Scelfo reminded the offensive line of the workouts in the sweltering Jackson gym.

He told them their whole journey was for this moment, it was time to block harder than they ever had before.

Ricard received the snap and took one step back. Again, here came defensive end Willie Evans, who zoomed past lineman Troy Kropog and roared toward Ricard. Ricard scurried away from the blitzing Evans, sprinting right, while Kropog lunged toward Evans, knocking him away from the quarterback. During a horizontal run across the 45-yard line, Ricard heaved the football toward a clump of helmets, some green, some maroon, hoping for a storybook ending.

Ricard's final pass was tipped at the goal line. It floated toward the back right corner of the end zone, right where Brian King was supposed to be standing. But in his eagerness to make something happen, King had crept toward the group of players at the goal line. The tipped ball sailed right over King's head. He desperately lifted his left hand, but it was too late. The ball landed on the grass, the pass incomplete, and the clock showed all zeros. Final score: Mississippi State 21, Tulane 14.

Soon after the final play, Jordan Ellis left the locker room and went into the hoards of Tulane fans, spotting his mother's blonde hair. The freshman linebacker hadn't seen his parents since their home and hometown had been destroyed. Ellis didn't play in the game, but he still beamed with pride. He had accomplished something just by being on that team; he had accomplished something by not quitting. The sobbing mother hugged her son and would not let go.

Spincer was exhausted from the efforts of making seven tackles, including the most important one of the night. Cordell knew that Spincer had played his hardest despite not having come up with the promised win. On the bus back to Ruston, they sat next to each other, and they both fell sound asleep.

After the game, Patti Terranova rode back to New Orleans with her friends, the Holts. She was still in her jersey. After gushing about Tulane's perseverance and Bubba's catch to keep the final drive alive, the car became quiet. And then, the trance of game night wearing off, Patti started crying as she moved closer to New Orleans and farther from Bubba. She would have to wait a week to put on her oversized jersey again, another seven days of nightmarish reality in New Orleans.

The weathered Coach Scelfo spoke to reporters who'd come from across the country, all wanting to get the story on New Orleans' team. That night, he told them: "I don't think that there's another team in America that is more united than ours right now. There's not one kid that lacks character. I'm extremely proud of the way they played."

CHAPTER 11

Victory

The night before Tulane's second game, a knock on the door shook Chris McGee out of his trance. It was Don Mahoney, the offensive line coach for the Green Wave. Mahoney is a teddy bear disguised as a football coach. With his Marine-like haircut and thunderous voice, he is a scary presence during football practice. But take the whistle off his neck, and Mahoney is a polite, gentle man, who speaks so softly that sometimes reporters' tape recorders don't pick up his quotes. This Friday night, the whistle was off.

Mahoney had lost his home in the hurricane. His family was safe but far away in Michigan. And though he missed his kids, he had a team of football players to take care of now. Mahoney knew his star left tackle was mentally strong; the kid had started 36 straight games and had dealt well with his feelings after the hurricane. But here came an emotional blitz; there was another hurricane on the radar, this one headed toward the Houston area. More specifically, toward Beaumont, Texas—McGee's hometown.

The existence of another hurricane seemed unfathomable. Players were still dealing with the aftermath of Katrina, and now Hurricane Rita was being predicted to hit the hometowns of 16 Tulane players, many of whom had already lost their college homes. Moreover, Tulane's second game, against Southern Methodist, was supposed to be on Saturday the 24th in Dallas, just 230 miles north of Houston. With Rita expected to hit the coast that afternoon, SMU changed the time of the game from 7 p.m. to 1 p.m. so that Tulane would be able to play the game and get back to Ruston should Rita continue north into Dallas that night. The team had traveled to Dallas by bus. They had made this trip before, after their stay at the Jackson State gymnasium.

On game day, dozens of McGee's family and friends united at the haven of Ford Stadium at SMU. There was Carolyn, his mother, a former Beaumont native now living in the Dallas area. There was Cassandra, his sister, who owned a home back in Beaumont. But his father, Willie Spears, wasn't in the stands; he was in his Chevy Suburban, stuck in maddening traffic headed north. Front bumpers inched closer to back bumpers as cars crept up the highway towards Dallas. The whole Houston area was evacuating. Spears, stuck in the gridlock, was near Irving, Texas, which was far enough away from SMU's campus that he feared he would miss the game altogether.

With 15 minutes left until kickoff, the temperature reached 87 degrees, while winds crept onto campus from the northeast at 21 miles per hour. Abrasive gusts loomed about three hours behind. Outside Ford Stadium, the same preppy students from the tailgate weeks earlier celebrated the game. The only difference was that today, Tulane was SMU's opponent.

SMU students dubbed their tailgate "Mustang Mardi Gras." SMU intended the name to be a show of support for Tulane, New Orleans, and the city's culture. There were drinks and funky music. A few fans tossed Mardi Gras beads to passersby. Girls flashed SMU's hand symbol when asked: "Show me your pony ears!" But the Mustang Mardi Gras seemed inappropriate given the fact that the real Mardi Gras was on life support.

Sprinkled throughout the SMU crowds were men, women, and children wearing green. Numerous Tulane families identified themselves with their names on the back of their jerseys, just like Patti Terranova. The Tulane golf team had been relocated to SMU, and though they were assimilating just fine on their new campus, they showed up to the game wearing green and ready to support Tulane.

The football team, cooped up in the locker room, was strangely confident despite the looming hurricane. Coach Scelfo demanded they ignore what they couldn't control. They couldn't control what would happen in the Houston area, but they could control what would happen in Dallas. And in Dallas, the players were comfortable; this was where they had spent the majority of the past month. More than Ruston, Dallas felt like home.

The image of Ricard's tipped pass was sewn on their minds as firmly as the numbers were on their jerseys. They had come very close to taking the Mississippi State game into overtime. In the end, they'd lost, but they'd also persevered, proving they could play some ball. Now, it was SMU that happened to be in their way; that's how Tulane felt as the team took the field. In the press box, a television showed a reporter in Beaumont, rain coming at him from every angle, his jacket hood flapping uncontrollably.

McGee, whose arm showcases a tattoo of the state of Texas, calmly got into position at the end of the line. He had been the left tackle since 2002, when he was a wide-eyed, red-shirted freshman with butterflies in his stomach. That season, and the season after, he blocked for quarterback J.P. Losman. Now McGee was in his second season blocking Ricard's blindside, an invaluable duty.

On the first snap against SMU, McGee began shuffling backward, when he suddenly froze, a red uniform whipping right past him. Ricard quickly completed the pass to Forté as McGee just hopped awkwardly in place. Then he fell to the ground. It was his ankle again; he had rolled it in the Mississippi State game. McGee hobbled toward the sideline, and Coach Scelfo met him a good five yards onto the field. The former and current offensive linemen walked side by side. Scelfo understood the unenviable pain his player was experiencing.

Troy Kropog dashed onto the field and took McGee's place on the drive, which Tulane went three-and-out. On the sideline, teammates came up to McGee, spewing encouragement, slapping his shoulder pads. Michael Parenton, the right guard, knew his buddy would be back out there. He had spent the previous year idolizing his elder teammate; Parenton knew McGee's threshold. After a series in 2004, McGee had walked toward the bench and plopped down as if he'd just finished a 15-round fight. Then, just as his backup had nervously put on a helmet, McGee guzzled a cup of water, jumped up from the bench, and hustled out for the next series. Parenton had laughed to himself, wondering how McGee could play so hard, series after series, game after game.

Just as Parenton had predicted, McGee was back at left tackle on Tulane's next possession, his ankle taped. Eventually, Tulane was forced to punt; this game's slow start gave it an eerie similarity to the Mississippi State game. But that feeling changed when Matt Harding, a Tulane freshman from the Dallas area, ripped the ball out of the punt returner's arms. Tulane's Carlis Jackson scooped it up, regaining possession in SMU's red zone. But Ricard's third-down strike to Terranova ricocheted off of him toward the ground. They decided to go for a field goal, which left most fans with little hope for a score; Tulane's kicking game was a carnival of ineptitude, and it had been for years. The kicker changed often because Tulane hadn't had much luck when it came to finding players who could consistently do the job. That day's kicker, Jacob Hartgroves, came out on the field. His field goal attempt hit the left upright. The game remained scoreless.

Ricard always seemed to need a few series to get into rhythm, but Scelfo didn't have a few series to waste. So when Tulane got the ball back, they ran against the susceptible SMU defense, first Jovon Jackson, then Forté, then more Jackson. On a nine-play drive, Tulane passed just once. Forté finally punctured the goal line, scoring the first touchdown; Tulane had its first lead of the season.

As Tulane's defense forced another SMU punt, Scelfo meticulously watched the game unfold. All week, he and his staff had prepared for SMU's scampering quarterback and bulldozing running back, as well as SMU's overachieving defense. And at this point, the plan was in effect. But there are no smiles when a game clock is ticking, not in the first half anyway, and definitely not when you're only up seven. Scelfo, showing no emotions, stood with his back slightly hunched as he marched up and down the sideline. His play card was stuffed in the front of his green practice shorts and gray long-sleeved shirt.

Beginning on Tulane's 29, Ricard marched his equal-opportunity offense down the field by completing six passes to five different receivers, with runs for Jackson and Forté spliced in. If there was ever a symbol that Tulane's offense was a system plugged with athletes, as opposed to a system built around its athletes, it was that drive.

Everything was going smoothly for the Green Wave. But then, Ricard threw a pass from the 10-yard line aimed at Damarcus Davis in the end zone corner. Instead of hitting the intended receiver, the pass landed in the hands of Rolando Humphrey, an SMU defensive back. Humphrey decided to gamble the 20 yards guaranteed from a touchback; he ran out of the end zone, tiptoed around some lunging Green Wave players near the sideline, and bolted. He stopped running a hundred yards later.

The stadium erupted as fans raised their pony ears. But Scelfo stood on the field, arms crossed, staring at a yellow flag. Kropog, filling in at right tackle on the play, was blocked from behind during the post-interception action. And so, instead of getting six points, SMU would have the ball at its own 6-yard line.

What happened next changed the course of the game. On paper, this was not supposed to be the game where the defensive line, largely an anonymous presence, turned into the Steel Curtain. SMU's quarterback, Jerad Romo, was a talented passer on the run, so Tulane often kept its linebackers stationed away from the line of scrimmage. Blitzing was basically out of the question. The pass rush had been delegated to the linemen. The defensive linemen weren't bad, but they usually didn't do much more than clog the middle, throwing an arm on a running back or a hand in a quarterback's face. But starting in the second quarter, for one glorious afternoon, the least heralded facet of Tulane's defense played better than it ever had before.

On a second-and-8 from SMU's 37, the pocket collapsed, and defensive end Taurean Brown charged in from the left side, forcing the quarterback to step up in the pocket. There, Romo was greeted by Avery Williams. He surged onto the jumpy quarterback, who finally fell into the grateful arms of defensive tackle Craig Morris. Brown, Williams, and Morris were largely unknown to those in the stands. While sportswriters furiously flipped through their media guides to identify the previously nameless defensive linemen, middle linebacker Cannon quickly ended the threat of a SMU drive by sacking their quarterback from behind.

After Route's muffed punt return in the Mississippi State game, Scelfo, constantly spicing up his game plan, gave return duties to Lucas, the senior safety. While Lucas wasn't the fastest player on the team, he had some football savvy and strength, and he was a veteran. Sure enough, after Lucas' roommate Cannon forced a fourth down with the sack, Lucas himself returned the punt 47 yards, giving Tulane its best field position all afternoon.

Although Tulane's offense had been less than reliable, Ricard came through on third-and-10 from the SMU 24; with just under three minutes in the first half, he zipped a perfectly timed pass to receiver Michael Batiste near the left sideline. Two plays later, Forté scored his second touchdown. Tulane was leading 14-0 with 1:14 left in the first half.

Those wearing green and sitting in Ford Stadium cheered, but up in the SMU press box, offensive coordinator Frank Scelfo was screaming a colorful play-by-play. On the play before the Batiste catch, for instance, a defensive lineman had swung around Kropog, ferociously drilling Ricard from the side for a sack. Frank Scelfo let the media and alumni sitting around him know how he felt, yelling, "Son of a bitch!" Then, as Forté broke free on his touchdown run, Frank narrated his movements: "Cut it back! Get in! Touchdown!"

As the game proceeded, Frank Scelfo cursed so often that he ran out of four-letter words. An older couple rooting for SMU and sitting near Scelfo's booth wished at that moment that they didn't have VIP seating. "He's something else," the husband said to his wife. "I've never heard it *this* bad," she answered. Oblivious to anything except his play calling, Scelfo continued to scream. Like his brother, this team had become his life. He cared deeply for his players, and his naturally fiery attitude spilled into his coaching. At practice, amid a cacophony of screaming coaches, his voice always seemed to reach the sky. He always had a joke in his arsenal and would back it up with a contagious laugh. During the tough times in Ruston, when a player was down, Frank would chirp: "Hey man, if you're goin' through hell, just keep goin'!"

At 2:38 p.m., Hurricane Rita, a Category 3 storm with 115 mile per hour winds, made landfall at Sabine Pass, Texas. Around the same time, the Green Wave went into halftime leading 14-0. Coach Scelfo stood in the end zone as his players jogged past, smacking each guy affirmatively on the back. During halftime, he told the offensive and defensive lines that, although they had been the reason behind their current lead, they would need to play even better if they wanted to win the game. Several players wondered, was Scelfo serious? Could the lines possibly play better? But the coach knew what it took to inspire his team; his point was to make sure they didn't get complacent. That lesson was fresh in their minds as they took the field to begin the second half.

The third quarter reverted to the typical back-and-forth seen in their first game. Both teams traded punts, and the quarter looked like a wash until DeMyron Martin, the SMU running back, made it into the Tulane red zone. SMU settled for a field goal, and with 4:49 left in the third quarter, the goose egg hatched into a three. Tulane was still in the lead, but now momentum was on SMU's side. The Green Wave couldn't afford to hang their helmet on anything they had already accomplished; they had nearly 20 minutes of football left to play. Scelfo had told his team over and over again that there was never a moment in a game where victory was certain, and that they had to keep playing their hardest. Sure enough, after the SMU score, Tulane began to march back down the field in a methodical 16-play drive that spilled into the fourth quarter. They mostly ran, but sprinkled in the drive were a couple brilliant Ricard passes. One was a 27-yard play action floater, thrown on the run, to Brian King, the freshman who had botched the final play against Mississippi State.

The Scelfo brothers went to their run game in the red zone, five in a row, all to Jovon Jackson. But Tulane couldn't cross the goal line and had to resort to its shaky special teams. Thankfully, Hartgroves made the kick this time. Tulane led 17-3 with 11:23 remaining in the game.

SMU's Jessie Henderson had return the previous two kickoffs for 59 and 27 yards. But Tulane changed their approach in an effort to minimize Henderson's damaging runs, kicking a bouncing line drive his way. It worked; the kick leaped out of his hands and into the arms of Tulane's Ray Boudreaux. And before Tulane's fans could finish celebrating the Tulane recovery, there was more to cheer about: a first-play touchdown pass, Ricard to Damarcus Davis. Coach Scelfo pumped the air with his fist. The score was now 24-3.

But the celebration didn't last long. SMU scored on the very next play when Henderson ran 88 yards for a kickoff return touchdown. In a game where both offenses had started off slow, suddenly a total of 17 points had been scored in 23 seconds.

Tulane punted on its next possession, and SMU opted for a new quarterback, hoping it would jolt their offense. Tony Eckert completed three of his first five passes. Just as Tulane started to worry, Eckert was sacked on a first down. But then he completed a second-down toss to the SMU 43. At third-and-5, they decided to pass again. This time, it went incomplete.

With 6:47 left in the game, SMU couldn't afford to punt; Tulane had proven it could gobble up the clock with its run game. So Eckert took the snap out of shotgun formation. On the right side off his line, the tackle and the guard corralled Tulane defensive tackle Frank Morton. Taurean Brown, the defensive end, cut inside, the left side of his jersey brushing against the back of one of these two blockers. That left only two people in the pocket; the quarterback and sack-happy Brown.

It was all over three plays later, when Ricard stepped back into his sealed pocket on third-and-3. From SMU'S 27, Ricard lofted a pass toward the goal line. The pass landed perfectly in the hands of Bubba Terranova. The touchdown, made with 5:03 remaining, gave Tulane a 31-10 lead. That would be the final score, even after the backups and the backups' backups got a little playing time.

When it was over, Tulane had tallied nine sacks, four of them on third down, and another two on fourth. Tulane physically and psychologically dominated SMU's offensive linemen: in total, 16 tackles for losses of 60 yards. Nine different receivers had caught passes that afternoon. Both running backs had made important runs. And the offensive line, with the big Texan on the end, played brilliantly. Every player on the team contributed to the victory. Coach Scelfo had challenged them, and they had responded.

But amidst the celebratory locker-room dancing, Rita's lurking presence reminded the players of what the victory couldn't do. It couldn't smother McGee's fear that his home-town was under siege at the very moment he was changing out of his uniform. But their win did remind them why they were even playing this season, and why they wouldn't quit.

Rita was initially the most intense tropical cyclone ever observed in the Gulf of Mexico; she became the fourth-most intense Atlantic Hurricane ever recorded. Total damage, mostly near the Texas-Louisiana border, exceeded $10 billion. There were 113 reported deaths. An estimated two million people lost electricity. In McGee's Beaumont, an estimated 25 percent of the trees were uprooted.

But for Tulane, the night of Rita's landfall was also the night of their first victory. Spincer later said of the win, "That revived things, gave us a boost. I remember watching the clock go down to 0:00 and lifting my hands to the sky. . . . It was so refreshing to get that feeling of hope and just to get something positive out of everything we had been working for."

CHAPTER 12

Homecoming

*F*or weeks the Tulane players' and coaches' only glimpses of their hometown came to them in the form of CNN footage. But on Friday, September 30, the team would return to New Orleans. They would stay there in preparation for their game; that weekend, they were going to host the Southeastern Louisiana Lions in Baton Rouge. The capital city was one of six sites that graciously allowed Tulane to host a game.

There wasn't a vacant hotel room within hours of New Orleans or Baton Rouge—they were still full of evacuees. By Wednesday, the team still didn't know where they would stay the night before the game. Coach Scelfo decided to pull some strings with English Turn Country Club. His home was on the property of English Turn, and though he feared the condition the area might be in—he'd heard that fires and looters had been rampant—he had no other options for housing his players.

Inside the bus on the drive in, players gazed out of their windows at the desolate streets. As the bus crawled past familiar places, they could make out only the skeleton of the city. Terranova remarked how much more stark reality seemed: "You can't get nothing from TV."

During a normal season, the Tulane team had always stayed in a hotel the night before a game, even when it was a home game. The night before a game is when teams harness their focus. It's when they break down that final piece of film or crystallize that final play in the game plan. But after seeing New Orleans for the first time with their own eyes since the hurricane, Tulane's focus could not solely be on the Southeastern Louisiana Lions. As the sun set on New Orleans that Friday, Parenton, Kropog, and tight end Jerome Landry sat on the clubhouse balcony. They spotted helicopters in the distance, most likely hovering above Landry's town of Chalmette. The floodwaters there had risen over 10 feet, and there had also been an oil spill. The three did not talk football. They talked about how comforting it was to be home, and how weird it was to be comforted considering the condition of the city. That night, Tulane's football team slept on air mattresses that Nancy Scelfo had spent the day inflating, and the players were thinking of home.

Scelfo returned to his house to find little damage; the hurricane had mostly affected his roof. But the neighborhood was desolate, and almost every tree had been snapped in half. "Thank God we won't have any more leaves in the yard," Scelfo said, "because I ain't got any more trees." He went into his kitchen and began brewing some coffee. His assistant coach, Bill D'Ottavio, interrupted him, a baffled look on his face. "Coach," he said, "you've got cows in your front yard."

The two men walked to the front door, and there on the lawn were at least 20 cows. They'd escaped from a local pasture.

On Saturday morning, the team loaded its bus for the hour-and-a-half drive to Baton Rouge's Tiger Stadium. The bus crossed the Crescent City Connection—the bridge over the Mississippi River—and drove through downtown New Orleans onto Interstate 10 West. There, on the right, was the Superdome, where this game was originally supposed to be played. A month earlier, thousands of sobbing and scared New Orleans residents had hidden inside the landmark. Now, the Superdome looked lonely, pathetic, and defeated.

The sight of the Superdome's dilapidated state messed with players' minds. "In this game we play, you have to be physically sharp, but more importantly, mentally sharp," Brandon Spincer said. "We passed the dome and the city was like a ghost town—that shit had an effect on me. It was in my head. We were mentally out of sync. That brought us back down. This was reality now: Everything is destroyed."

Also difficult to deal with was the fact that the game against SLU was originally scheduled as Tulane's homecoming. The word never had more resonance. Though the official homecoming events had been suspended—how could you have a homecoming queen when you didn't have a student body?—thousands of Tulane alums and supporters united in Baton Rouge. It was a peculiar setting, Tulane fans holding court outside Louisiana State University's Tiger Stadium. It didn't look right; the two schools were rivals, often playing each other in heated football, basketball, and baseball games. But in a time where Louisianans were accustomed to welcoming evacuees into their homes, it was fitting. And so, before kickoff, the Tulane community drank cold Abita beer and talked about the exciting win at

Southern Methodist and tried to avoid mentioning the hurricane. One fan carried around a homemade sign that read: "Tulane Lives."

Amid the alumni and the Tulane students currently spending the semester elsewhere, there were plenty of familiar faces around: Scott Cowen, the university president; Tommy Manzella, the former Tulane baseball player and minor leaguer, who'd lost everything in Chalmette; David Melius, the displaced owner of Bruno's, a Tulane watering hole around since 1934; Les East, the veteran Louisiana sportswriter, who prior to the storm had thought he'd seen it all.

One familiar face not in attendance was Chris Dawson, the fourth-string quarterback. For each game, Tulane had to chose only a certain number of players to travel, and this was the first game of the year that Dawson didn't make the cut. He used the time to visit his girlfriend, whom he hadn't seen since the storm. She was a Tulane student spending the displaced semester in Texas, so Dawson made the seven-hour trip from Ruston to Austin, planning to return on Monday before afternoon meetings. He assumed the team would have Sunday off: Scelfo had instituted "Victory Sundays," which meant the team had Sunday off if they were victorious on Saturday. A loss, and the boys would have Sunday meetings and weight-lifting sessions.

Dawson figured this game was a sure-thing victory, as did his teammates. The Lions were a Division-II football team and considered a lesser opponent; that's why the game had been scheduled as homecoming, to ensure that alums had a reason to cheer. Win or lose, Tulane was driving back to Ruston on Saturday night. Dawson planned to drive back Monday morning and not miss a thing.

At 2:30 p.m. on Saturday, amid sweltering, 90-degree heat, the Green Wave took the field in their white road uniforms. A compact disc played the Tulane fight song over the loud speakers. Tulane won the coin toss, demanded the football, and before the tailgaters had turned off their grills, Ricard was driving his offense down field, the SLU defense only a minor inconvenience.

Ricard seemed to have an extra second in the pocket or extra zip on his ball, as he easily scattered the field with completions. Everyone got a turn. His first pass of the day was a 10-yarder to Preston Brown; he completed his next seven attempts to four other players before turning to Jovon Jackson. Jackson had the nickname "Shaq," because during his childhood, he once shattered a youth basketball backboard ala Shaquille O'Neal. Whenever Tulane needed a hard-earned yard, they went with Shaq, their quintessential punisher. On his first carry, second-and-3 from the SLU 12, Jackson chugged up the middle for six yards. On the next play, he went for six more, landing in the end zone with a couple of Lions on his back.

But after that first score, something seemed to take over the Tulane players, something that had to do with everything they'd been through and everything they'd seen that weekend. What suddenly seemed to take over the team, what they'd so far been able to shake off but now could not, was fatigue. It first struck the Tulane offense. Their next five possessions ended in a punt. The sixth ended via interception. Then they punted again, futilely ending the first half, which had begun with such promise.

The Tulane defense, though, was vibrant. They entered the game No. 1 in the nation in total defense. And for the third-straight game, they held their opponent scoreless in the first half, entering the locker room up 7-0.

But Coach Scelfo knew. He saw fatigue creeping through his team. If they were going to win that game, Scelfo and his staff had to keep his players positive and upbeat. Having seen their hometown firsthand had changed them; they had a harder time focusing on a football game when the reality of their homes was so vivid, and suddenly so close. But just like in the previous game during Hurricane Rita, Scelfo told his team to focus only on what they could control. They had to let go of whatever was beyond their power to change.

The third quarter began much like the first, except that this time, it was SLU moving the ball. The teams seemed to have switched places; Scelfo stood on the sideline and watched SLU quarterback Trey Willie pick apart his No. 1 defense the same way Ricard had the SLU defense in the first half. In fact, Willie completed all eight of his attempts, just as Ricard had. It was clear to Scelfo that the fatigue that had plagued the offense had now spread to his defense. For the first time all year, the boys looked consistently sloppy.

Three plays in particular showed that this was not just the typical miscue Tulane's defense had experienced before; this was a much bigger problem. And worse, each of the three plays occurred on third down. The first was when Spincer misjudged a tackle attempt right at the first down marker, allowing an opponent to scamper free. The second was when SLU's offensive line smothered Tulane's line, and Willie, on a passing play, ran for an unfettered 18 yards. The third example was when Willie dragged defensive tackle Antonio Harris several yards, then shook him off, and then lobbed a touchdown pass to Felton Huggins, who sped past the lethargic safety Tra Boger. "Man on man," Scelfo said later, "they were just whipping us."

Huggins tied the game with 9:07 left in the third quarter. Tulane, rattled, earned one first down but couldn't muster any more. They were again forced to punt.

Somewhere in Texas, Dawson continued to punch the buttons on his car radio, hoping to snatch a broadcast of the Tulane game. But all he got was country music. He decided to call backup kicker Michael Sager, who also hadn't dressed for the game.

"What's the score, man?" asked Dawson, at that point only wondering by how much his team was winning. When Sager told him the game was tied, Dawson said, "What the hell is going on? We ought to be killing these guys!"

On the field, Ricard was just as dumbfounded—and embarrassed. The kid with NFL dreams couldn't beat a Division II defense? So he came out firing, his prettiest ball a 48-yarder to Brian King. On third-and-8 on SLU's 19, Ricard had four receivers, a staple of the Scelfo offense. Ricard, in shotgun formation, looked to his left and saw the running back Forté. The quarterback sent him to the line of scrimmage as a receiver. Now there were five receivers and not one blocker in the backfield. Ricard spotted receiver Cary Koch and calmly threw him a touchdown pass to take a 14-7 lead into the fourth quarter.

But with a Division I-A swagger, SLU's Willie threw his second touchdown with 13:13 left, and the game was tied. Worse yet, Tulane had begun to unravel; Frank Morton received a penalty for unsportsmanlike conduct and was ejected from the game. Although the game was tied, SLU had the momentum and, it seemed, the composure of a winner. But Tulane had Izzy Route, the cornerback who, at 5-foot-9, gave his all at every opportunity.

As the returner on the game-opening kickoff, Route had been smashed to the ground, and a throbbing pain had shot south from his head down his spine. It even hurt Route to lift his head. He spent some time on the sideline, reassuring the trainers he could play. He was put in to catch the post-touchdown kickoff. Once the ball was in his hands, he did what he does best: he ran down he field, dodging defenders, and suddenly he was alone. As he sprinted down field, he began feeling dizzy and worried whether or not he could make it all the way to the end zone.

At the SLU 3-yard-line, a Lion latched onto Route from behind, but Route carried him into the end zone. The 97-yard touchdown return gave Tulane a 20-14 lead (the extra point was blocked). After such an amazing run, Scelfo joked that for the next game, he would bring a hammer and knock Route on the helmet to replicate the opening kickoff hit—whatever it took for Route to duplicate his performance.

The teams then traded punts several times. With 6:25 left in the game, SLU was down just six points to a Division I-A opponent, and SLU had the ball on that opponent's 34-yard line. Tulane's defense worked hard, but it was clear that fatigue had them fighting just to breathe. The Lions went short on their first three plays, hoping to puncture their way to a first down. But this strategy brought them to the ultimate predicament; it was fourth-and-6 on Tulane's 30—too far for a field goal, too close to punt, and too little time left on the clock to do anything except, of course, go for it.

With 4:49 left in the best game of his life, Willie threw a short pass to Jeffrey Howard, who eluded two defenders before diving cornerback Jeremy Foreman knocked him off his feet. Cannon had simultaneously jumped on Howard's back, twisting Howard's body in mid-air. Spincer, looming near the play, looked at the first-down marker. Howard, on the ground, was a good two yards away. The defense, though terribly tired, had done its job.

The Tulane offense, which hadn't made a first down in nearly a quarter, now had only the simple task of not blowing it. Unfortunately, it looked like that might be a task Ricard couldn't handle. He threw consecutive incompletes from his 26-yard line. The botched second down, though, proved valuable. On the play, Ricard looked for Terranova cutting toward the middle of the field. The pass was tipped at the line, but Tulane coaches noticed SLU's anticipation for the short pass, Ricard's weapon that Saturday. So on third down, Ricard baited the defense again. Damarcus Davis cut to the inside, preparing for a short pass, and Ricard pump-faked his throwing arm toward him. A cornerback, a safety, and a linebacker all converged on Davis. Terranova stood a few yards from Davis, selling a potential block. Just as the defenders approached Davis, Terranova took off like a sprinter down the right sideline. Ricard launched a pass, which Bubba caught in stride at the 48-yard line.

All 11 Lions were behind him. Numerous Tulane players took off down the sideline, parallel to Terranova. Others waved towels and screamed. Terranova crossed the goal line, held the ball up in the air, and tripped over his own tired feet, falling onto the turf. Tulane nailed the two-point conversion, and with 3:38 left, they led 28-14.

Just as Scelfo had preached at halftime, his team persevered with a game on the line. The Lions, playing for pride, marched in the waning minutes. They scored a touchdown on the game's final play, losing 28-21. It was another Willie touchdown pass, his third, capping his 38-for-54 passing day, good for 268 yards.

Minutes before the final whistle, during Terranova's big play, Tulane had been pumped and full of energy. But after the final whistle, as the weary team walked off the field, not one player smiled. This had to be a first for a winning team. They were proud of their accomplishment; they had prepared all week to win this game. But they knew they hadn't won this game so much as they hadn't lost it. A lesser team from a lesser division pushed Tulane around for much of the game. Man for man, they'd been whipped.

And there were so many glaring issues they knew needed to be addressed. For instance, after Jackson's rushing touchdown way back on the first drive, the Tulane run game had been stymied, managing only 38 total yards from Jackson and Forté combined. Ricard had thrown two touchdowns, but also two interceptions. And the defense, except on one or two occasions, hadn't made key stops. If they had these kinds of issues against a Division II school, they didn't want to see what happened the next time they faced quarterbacks in their own conference. As Tulane walked off the field that day, they felt more negative feelings than positive ones.

For everything that the coaches thought they could control—play calling, substitutions, strategy—there was one thing they could not control: it was Game No. 3, and the team was already fatigued. The effects of weeks of travel, displacement, stress, and sleeplessness—not to mention the psychological repercussions plaguing most players—had finally shown up that Saturday. And for all they tried, that fatigue made it hard for them to enjoy Victory Sunday, too.

CHAPTER 13

Motivation

*T*ulane players pushed the issue of fatigue to the backs of their minds as they entered the locker room during halftime the following week. Their performance during the first half of their game against the Houston Cougars led them to believe that the previous week's struggle against SLU had only been an aberration. They were currently tied with Houston, 7-7, playing in the late afternoon in Lafayette, Louisiana, Tulane's home city for a day.

Tulane had entered the Houston game having allowed just 73.7 rushing yards per game. Against Houston during the first half, Tulane had allowed 63 rushing yards, which was impressive. But the second half proved to be a lot more trouble, and the issue of fatigue crept its way back toward the forefront of the team's thinking.

In the end, Houston's running backs steam-rolled Tulane's defense. Ryan Gilbert knocked away defenders, running for 104 yards in the second half alone and scoring twice. During the final two quarters, the Cougars tallied 185 rushing yards and four rushing touchdowns. Tulane lost 35-14, and fell to 2-2 on the season.

Anthony Cannon, still wearing his grass-stained uniform, lingered outside the locker room after Coach Scelfo's speech. Cannon led Tulane with 14 tackles that night, but he knew he could have made more. His teammates definitely could have made more. Cannon was humble, pinning the loss on himself and on the defense. But he was also worried why it had happened.

In the coming days, as Tulane studied the film of the loss to Houston, the reality of what was happening became clear. They knew about the constants in college football: every team enters the season in fine physical shape after a structured preseason; every team has its own community and campus, with familiar classrooms, dorm rooms, locker rooms, and weight rooms; every team plays at least half of its games in its home city. Tulane was the lone team in the country without these three constants, the only team with the deck stacked against them, predisposing them to loss long before they ever reached that week's field.

During the weeks in Dallas, when football was an afterthought, the time Tulane spent practicing and lifting weights had shrunk. So had some of the players. Senior safety Darren Sapp had lost 10 pounds, weight he'd gained in muscle during his first three seasons of training. Jordan Ellis, the freshman, had lost nearly 30 pounds. In a sport largely based on physicality, Tulane was playing catch-up during the week, which meant they were literally trying to catch up to running backs on Saturdays.

But the team prided itself on its mental strength, its spirit. The idea of mental toughness, drilled into them by Scelfo, got Tulane through the endless days in Jackson and Dallas. Mental toughness was why they were still playing for Tulane when, at the time, there wasn't even a Tulane. But the road of perseverance had potholes. The stress began to wear down even the most mentally tough players. For instance, there was one day when Cannon went to the equipment room—the large closet where John Mendow organized all of Tulane's gear at Tech's Assembly Center—looking for some extra socks. Mendow explained to him that there weren't any extra socks; there was only enough to give each player one pair. Cannon didn't believe him, but Mendow insisted he didn't have any. Mendow then walked out of the room and down the hall, off to his next task. Cannon exploded; he lost his temper and threw his helmet at Mendow. He missed, but the helmet smacked the wall, the sound reverberating through the hallway.

The coaching staff was having an equally difficult time dealing with stress. Frank Scelfo, for example, occasionally blew up at Dawson, the happy-go-lucky quarterback who never played. Chris Scelfo dealt with the stress by eating more than he ever had during his offensive line days back in college.

Some of the players found it difficult to concentrate in the classroom. Even talented football players sometimes can't play college football because they can't handle the college part. Balancing classes with positional meetings while studying textbooks and playbooks can be demanding. Couple that with the pressure to succeed on game day, along with Tulane's added challenges brought about by the hurricane, and what you have is a situation that is, at the very least, incredibly draining for players. Terranova—his mother away, his car totaled, and his home destroyed—could seldom focus on schoolwork, and his grades in two classes lingered around Fs. When your football season is on the fritz, it's tough to embrace geology.

The Saturday after the Houston game, a national television audience tuned in to watch the Green Wave. A sign at a Jiffy Lube on Highway 167 read "Welcome to Ruston, ESPN. Go Tulane." Tulane's lone game in Ruston was against the Texas El-Paso Miners and their potent Conference USA offense. UTEP's quarterback, Jordan Palmer, was a dead-ringer for an NFL Pro Bowler, partly because Jordan was the younger brother of 2002 Heisman Trophy winning quarterback Carson Palmer. Ricard was up for the challenge, at least early on that night when he heaved a 64-yard touchdown to Preston Brown, who had emerged as Tulane's go-to receiver. Then, with 3:17 left in the second quarter, Ricard hit Terranova for a touchdown. Tulane trailed just 17-14.

As ESPN commentators talked about Tulane's post-Katrina hardships and their perseverance, home viewers nonetheless saw the storm's negative effects on the team's performance, too. After the Terranova touchdown, the Tulane defense forced a punt. If Tulane could score on this drive, they could either tie or take the lead into halftime. But as the punt dropped from the Louisiana sky, Tulane's Josh Lumar stuck his hands up like a basketball player grabbing a rebound: a kick-returning faux pas. The ball bounced off his palms and into UTEP's possession on Tulane's 35. Palmer, as poised a passer as his Cincinnati Bengal brother, hit receiver Johnny Lee Higgins on the first two plays, the second a 22-yard touchdown pass.

Despite Lumar's blunder and Tulane's sudden 10-point deficit, the Tulane players were determined to show the nation their famous resilience. The offense marched from their own 11 all the way to UTEP's 14. With 46 seconds left in the half, Ricard pump-faked and spotted a seam. But when a running Ricard crossed the 10-yard line, Troy Collavo smashed into him from the side. Ricard had been hit plenty of times with the football in more vulnerable positions, but on this play, he lost his concentration and the ball sputtered out of his possession. UTEP's Josh Ferguson recovered. Palmer knelt on the ensuing snap, and he jogged into the locker room up 10 points.

Later in the third quarter, Ricard hit Brown again for a touchdown, and then Tulane, down 24-21, got the ball back on a punt. Ricard completed a pass to Damarcus Davis, but Ferguson knocked the ball from the receiver's hands. UTEP's Jeremy Jones scooped it up and jetted 25 yards for a touchdown. Tulane wouldn't score again. Mental mistakes cost them a winnable game. They finished the game with a 2-3 record and little to build upon.

One day the next week, Tulane's reserve running back and linebacker Ryan Bewley left a class he didn't want to take. It was almost November, but the effects of August's storm were apparent daily. Like his Green Wave teammates, Bewley was lonely, exhausted, and discouraged. He sat at an outdoor table on Tech's campus and reminisced about the days when everything seemed to be in Tulane's favor. Now Tulane had slipped past Division-II SLU, and then let two conference games slip out of their hands. "I just don't think we were 100 percent," he later said. "It's like we were fighting with blurred vision."

The Tulane players had enough perspective to realize that living in a hot dorm room was better than spending the semester in a FEMA trailer. Playing football was a luxury, and they could have chosen to cancel their season. They were grateful even when dinner was nachos and burgers, or there was a line for the bench press; to complain about their living conditions seemed wrong when compared to those of other hurricane survivors. But when they compared their situation to those of their opponents, they couldn't help but feel sorry for themselves. They missed their campus, the social life that buzzed on and around it. Friends, family, and professors were elsewhere. Girlfriends were scattered across the country, taking classes at other schools. The days in Ruston felt longer, and the sweltering nights were loathsome. With little energy and little to do, the players often just loafed around Caruthers Hall. The hallways were dirty and dark. Mysterious splotches dotted the walls, and bugs infested the rooms.

One day, Route spotted an attractive young coed on campus. The sly cornerback, never afraid to make a move, promptly flirted with his Tech classmate. She was hesitant at first, but who could resist the charm of Izzy Route? He asked her if she would like to come over and hang out some time. She smiled and asked where he lived. "Caruthers," he told her.

"Oh, no," she said. Although many of the building's residents not associated with the Tulane team were gracious and grateful to have shelter, there were a few who were shady, who seemed to spend too much time drinking and getting into trouble. These particular residents, evacuees from around the state, had caused Caruthers to develop a bad reputation on Tech's campus

Jordan Ellis witnessed one instance of this kind of problem. He was in his room one day when Anthony Scelfo, Frank's son and Chris' nephew, walked in. Anthony had spent the previous night at his parents' place, and upon his return to Caruthers, he found a cell phone on his bed. There was a missed call, so Anthony dialed the number. The guy on the other end was downstairs in the dorm. The man found his friend, who the phone belonged to, and the two went up to retrieve the phone from Anthony.

The man who owned the phone fumbled around the room. He held a cup of beer in his hand. It was 11 a.m. "Why was your phone was in my room?" Anthony Scelfo asked.

"I was drunk, and I didn't know what I did!" the man answered. Anthony and the man started arguing. Another teammate went downstairs to get a police officer on duty. Meanwhile, two women wandered upstairs. After listening to the argument, one of the women said, "He's always drunk. And he slept in your bed last night!" After everyone calmed down, the drunks returned downstairs and Anthony put his sheets in the washer.

Later in the day, Ellis and Anthony retold the story to teammate James Dillard. "I saw that dude!" Dillard told them. "He knocked on my door at 4 a.m. He was walking down the hall, butt naked!"

○ ○ ○

On a calm October night, Anthony Cannon sat on his dorm mattress wondering where the season would go from then on. Could his team bounce back, pick up a win or two, and recapture the confidence they'd had after the SMU game? Or was the fatigue they'd been working through just too great—had they been punched just one too many times? Coach Scelfo had told them over and over again that this season wasn't about winning or losing; it was about perseverance, about punching back. It was about learning to appreciate what you still had. Cannon said of the season so far, "It makes you more grateful for the things you had back at Tulane. When I do get back, I'm just going to lie on the ground and hug the earth. Hopefully, none of the flood bacteria on the ground will get in my skin."

For Cannon, the lesson of appreciating what you once had and what you still have was coming through loud and clear. But Scelfo still sometimes spotted players moping during practices, lost in their thoughts and memories. Scelfo made it a point to sit with his players during lunch so that he could gauge their emotions, keeping an eye out for those who needed a boost. He would often give individual players mini-pep talks, asking them why they played. Each player had a different answer, but the point was they did have a reason—they only needed to be reminded of it.

Some of the guys played for New Orleans and its residents, hoping their perseverance would inspire the city's natives. Others played for more specific people. Bubba Terranova played for his mother. She told him again and again that she lived for the weekend, lived to watch her son fulfill his dream. Football became her refuge, and she then became a refuge for her son; whenever things seemed their most dire, his cell phone would ring. It was always mom calling. The Terranovas had lost nearly everything in the storm, but Bubba had his football team and Patti had football games. Knowing how much the games mattered to her made Bubba play his hardest every week.

Family also motivated Brandon Spincer; he played for his children, who were spending the fall with their mother in Houston. Being away from Branisha and Brandon Jr. was especially hard on him. For Spincer, Sundays were the toughest. Those were the days that, back in New Orleans, he would spend the whole day with his children. They would go to church, swing home to see Grandma and Grandpa, and then head to

Chuck E. Cheese. Spincer's children became the motivation behind every bench press, every class, every exam, and every fourth quarter. He knew that whatever he accomplished in Ruston would help his kids in the coming years, whether it be an opportunity to play at the NFL level or a meaningful degree from Tulane.

Spincer's teammates understood his passion and fed off it. Though every senior was a captain that season, Spincer emerged as the captain's captain. Ask any player on the team to name the team leader among them, and the answer was always the same. That fall, Coach Scelfo told Spincer there would always be a spot available on his staff if Spincer ever decided to become a coach.

The irony was that Spincer was seldom vocal. He didn't seek out popularity or demand the spotlight. He simply worked harder than anyone else in practice and in the weight room, and when he saw the opportunity to motivate his teammates, he'd calmly do so. He had once struggled to survive at Tulane because of academic ineligibility; now he was helping his teammates survive, and it was his children who fueled his focus.

But no matter what the specific motivation, everyone on the team played at least in part for each other. Their commitment to the team went far beyond the typical teamwork sound bite most other teams gave at Monday press conferences. For Tulane, teamwork was real, and they were further bonded by the storm and its aftermath, by how they lived through it together. They cooked for each another on George Foreman grills; cornerback Carlis Jackson was often the chef. They serenaded each other with popular rap songs. They sat around into the wee hours, telling tall tales about fishing or hunting. On every other football team in the country, players lived all around campus, uniting solely for football events. But the players on the Tulane team were always together, discovering who they were underneath the uniforms.

The challenge now, after two straight losses, was to convert that camaraderie into momentum—and into wins.

CHAPTER 14

Quarterback

Lester Ricard was a 6-foot-5 amalgam of pious and pompous. His father, Lester Sr., was a popular minister in the quaint town of Denham Springs, Louisiana, where the bustle in downtown involved mostly antiquing. Lester Jr., whose voice is as soft as a breeze, often punctuated his sentences with gospel. While at Tulane, he regularly made the 86-mile drive home on Sunday mornings to sit in the pews with his mother. But he made the drive in a white Cadillac Escalade, proclaiming his quarterback status every mile from the fast line. Ricard talked the talk, but he walked the proverbial walk with a swagger.

Ricard had been a high school football phenomenon at Amite High. In his junior and senior years, he completed 244-of-434 attempts for 3,765 yards and 40 touchdowns. He was ranked as the nation's No. 5 high school quarterback by the recruiting web site Rivals.com. He decided to play football at

Louisiana State University, the Southeastern Conference stalwart.

Ricard paraded into Baton Rouge, but soon found his weaknesses dwarfing his athleticism. He wasn't always focused. He was inconsistent. He was cocky, but not confident. As an incoming freshman in 2002, he'd held the future of LSU football in his hands, but soon found himself holding only a clipboard. He wanted more playing time, so the prized recruit sped down Interstate 10 to New Orleans.

Because the rules said so, Ricard had to sit out Tulane's 2003 season, his first on campus. That year, he watched the wily J.P. Losman lead the offense with his crazy legs and slingshot arm. Losman went on to become a finalist for the Johnny Unitas Award, given to the country's top quarterback. In the spring, the Buffalo Bills drafted him in the first round. But Ricard watched him from the stands on Saturdays and thought to himself, "I can do that." He yearned to prove himself on the field, wanting to shrug the stigma of being the kid who couldn't cut it at LSU.

In Ricard's first year as Tulane's quarterback, 2004, he ranked 11th in the country in passing efficiency. In 2005, he was poised to fulfill his dream of becoming the next great Green Wave quarterback. He'd had another success, this one off the field: he'd found a best friend.

Michael Parenton, the offensive lineman, had become Ricard's best friend and confidant. The friendship began in 2003, Ricard's transfer year at Tulane. It was a Wednesday and Frank Scelfo was on the phone with Parenton, a high school recruit out of E.D. White High. Back in Thibodaux, they remembered the high school playoff game, when that lanky LSU recruit tore up their defense. Sure enough, Ricard was lounging that day in Scelfo's office; he spent so much time there, he was known to fall asleep on the couch. When Ricard realized Scelfo was speaking with an E.D. White player, Ricard grabbed the phone, introduced himself, and began talking trash. It was light-hearted, nothing biting, and Parenton started laughing at the goofball quarterback on the other end. Parenton signed with Tulane, and in 2004, his red-shirt season, he and Ricard slowly became buddies.

Some teammates thought it was an unusual pairing because of their different personalities and backgrounds, but the two eventually thought of each other as family. When Parenton arrived in a room, Ricard would often say, "Here's my brother from another mother!" Parenton would shout back, "Kin with different skin!"

Often in college, and especially on football teams, friendships can be temporary and flimsy. These relationships are often built in the weight room, not at the dinner table, and they're often based on superficialities. But Ricard and Parenton shared a genuine and sturdy friendship. Parenton even discovered the quarterback's secret nickname from back home: "Sparky." Said Ricard of the friendship: "It's one of the relationships where, whoever is on their deathbed, you want the other there. That's how much we care about each other."

Parenton's family moved to Uptown New Orleans when Parenton began attending Tulane, and Ricard spent much of the summer of 2005 there at his home. During the days, the duo would walk over to campus to participate in off-season work-outs, debating which *Batman* movie was the best, among other equally pressing topics.

That summer, weeks before Hurricane Katrina made land-fall, the two headed south to Thibodaux. There, every summer, former Saints quarterback Archie Manning hosted the Manning

Passing Academy, a yearly event which featured Manning's famous sons as counselors: Indianapolis Colts quarterback Peyton and New York Giants quarterback Eli. The campers varied from high school backups to elite college quarterbacks, such as LSU's JaMarcus Russell and Tulane's Ricard. Parenton would sometimes slip away from family and friends and watch the Manning Passing Academy from the bleachers.

Ricard and Parenton would prove themselves to be the two biggest goofballs on that 2005 Tulane team. In fact, they sometimes came across as giggling schoolchildren, the only ones in on an inside joke. "He's goofier," Parenton said of Ricard. "He's definitely under the realization that he's goofier. He thinks he can dance as well as Michael Jackson. Not even close. And any time an offensive lineman can dance better than you, you're in trouble."

Ricard at times seemed so goofy that some even questioned his seriousness. But he cherished his role on the offense. Before each opening kickoff in 2005, Ricard would find a quiet spot, away from the pregame frenzy, and silently shed tears. His emotions simply overwhelmed him; he loved the game of football and cherished each game, especially because the games very well could have been canceled that year. He once joked that, had the season been canceled, he would have suffered a nervous breakdown. Based on his reaction to each game, it was clear that there was more than a little truth behind his joke.

Despite his need to play, the hurricane-altered season was a whirlwind one for the quarterback. He was, at times, an emotional mess. His home hadn't been severely damaged by the storm, but the trauma of the hurricane was real, and he was an emotional person to begin with. Ricard had had permanent tears in his eyes those first days in Dallas, his uncle missing, his family and girlfriend far away, and the CNN footage tattooed on his mind. But he had God; every night, in the balmy Ruston dorm room, he would read five or six chapters from the New Testament. He also had his best friend Parenton, and he had football.

He'd struggled in his performance against Houston and had been benched, but he'd made significant improvement the following week against UTEP. The biggest difference was on third down; against Houston, he'd gone 2-for-9, but against the Miners he'd gone 11-for-18. All three of his touchdown passes came on third down, too. UTEP coach Mike Price had even said, "[Ricard] is capable of playing with any quarterback in the country."

The Green Wave, at 2-3, was trodden. It was obvious that stamina would be an issue in every game for the rest of the year. The defense was fatigued, and many felt that the only hope for a better season stood behind the center: the multifaceted and multifaced Ricard.

o o o

On Wednesday, October 19, Coach Scelfo addressed his team, each player on one knee, at the Louisiana Tech practice field. He said, "I know there's somebody out there that did something wrong," meaning that there had to be something upsetting the team's karma. It was the only way to explain the latest news; Hurricane Wilma was headed toward the Orlando area that weekend—the same weekend Tulane was supposed to play the Orlando-based University of Central Florida. School officials had decided to push Saturday's game to Friday. Suddenly, Tulane lost a day in its preparations for the game.

Even worse, Tulane would have to fly to Orlando on the same day it would play, and then fly back to Louisiana immediately after the game.

It should be noted that, in general, college football teams never travel on the day of a game; in many ways, it puts the team at a disadvantage long before the opening kickoff. For Tulane, however, this trip would be the third time that season that the team would have to travel on a game day. In fact, it would be their fourth time if one counts the hour-and-a-half drive from New Orleans to Baton Rouge to play SLU.

The news was enough to make John Mendow choke on his Skoal. Game-day travel meant that on Friday, the equipment manager without an equipment staff would be awake for 24 straight hours during what he described as "an absolute nightmare." The Friday game inconvenienced Patti Terranova, too, but she wouldn't miss it for anything—even if the game were being played in the eye of Hurricane Wilma. The schoolteacher made arrangements for her Friday absence with her principal, and on Thursday evening she began driving east to Florida. Along with friend Bridget Holt, lineman Scott Holt's mother, the two drove through the dark night, stopping occasionally to rest their eyes or grab something to eat.

Tulane had an equally long trip ahead of them. Come Friday, they were up before sunrise on a day that wouldn't end until a couple hours before sunrise the next day. At 7:15 that morning, the team united inside the campus dining hall, where a handful of Tech undergrads crammed for morning tests. Football players slowly chewed on bacon strips. Twenty-two minutes later, three charter busses arrived, and 96 players, coaches, and staff stepped aboard, each wearing a white short-sleeved collared shirt featuring a small Tulane logo.

For many football players, game day is like Christmas; they wake up in the morning, body tingling, ready to tear something open. But this day, Tulane would have to sit in front of the tree for hours, maddeningly watching Santa's milk curdle. First was the half-hour drive from Ruston to the airport in Monroe. Then everyone and all the equipment had to go through security. Finally, after boarding the plane, Southwest charter flight 8042 took off toward Orlando. It landed at 10:42 a.m. Kickoff wasn't until 7 p.m.

They ate dinner at 1:30 p.m.—spaghetti, white rice, green beans, and grilled chicken. Between bites, players spoke to each other, trying to conjure up some semblance of the typical game-day meal.

Coach Scelfo had been sick all week. He remained congested on game day. At 3:10 p.m., he waited along with the rest of his team to load the busses. Tulane took another 30-minute bus ride, this time to the stadium. The windshield wipers swooshed methodically, sweeping away Wilma's preliminary raindrops.

In the stands before kickoff, Patti, wearing her jersey, scoured the area for familiar faces. With the game having been pushed to a workday, with a third hurricane on its way, and with the Orlando trip being one of the farther trips to begin with, Patti estimated there were as many Tulane fans at this game as there were Tulane players. So Patti determined she would just have to cheer louder.

In the locker room with 10 minutes until kickoff, each player sat in front of his locker in a gleaming white uniform. The only sound you could hear was athletic tape peeling off a roll. Dennis Polian, the director of football operations, briskly walked into the locker room and blew a whistle. On cue, every player hopped up, convening at the front of the room, each of them down on one knee. Coach Scelfo came to the front of the group to speak.

"It's time for us to even this one up," he said. "Let's even this one up. We've got to focus on every single time that ball is snapped. Every single time. Guys, we've got the better team. We've been here before. Now we need to finish. We need to reward ourselves with great effort, passion, enthusiasm—for four quarters. If we focus and finish the job . . . if we focus and finish the job, we're going to walk off this field victorious. Do not let anything stand in your way of being successful tonight. Do not let anything stand in your way of being successful. Have fun, but have fun with a focus and a purpose. And that's to do what?"

"Win!"

"To do what?"

"WIN."

Scelfo's words seemed to have struck a cord, but it took Tulane just two plays to make a mental mistake. After a first-down run, Ricard had five receivers spread on second down. The pocket was as empty as the Tulane fan section. Ricard spotted Terranova cutting into the middle of the field, and the quarterback flung a lead pass. The pass was aimed at Terranova's destination spot, but upon his arrival there, a defender was already in place, waiting. UCF's Frisner Nelson made the interception, Tulane's first turnover of the game.

UCF notched a field goal; Tulane punted again. And that's when running back Kevin Smith, who'd already been one of Scelfo's concerns going into the game, introduced himself to the Tulane defenders. From the Tulane 42, the speedy Smith angled left, where UCF blockers smothered Tulane's Mason and Boger, creating a gaping hole. Smith gobbled up green 10 yards at a time until Lucas shoved him out of bounds at the 9. Before Smith could catch his breath—and as the defenders huffed and puffed—his number was called again. Smith bulldozed right through the middle of the Tulane defense, and UCF quickly jumped to a 10-0 lead.

Tulane tried to drive the same way, shoving running backs down the defenders' throats. On this ensuing drive, Tulane backs accumulated 41 ground yards. Ricard put the finishing touch on the drive with a play action zip to Bobby Hoover, the senior tight end, who caught the pass over a linebacker's shoulder while tumbling into the end zone grass.

UCF notched another field goal, making it 13-7, but Ricard quickly snatched the lead, lobbing a perfect ball 44 yards to Preston Brown's outstretched arms for a touchdown. Brown had now scored touchdowns in three consecutive games. Tulane's sideline began to buzz.

After a UCF punt, Terranova caught a slant pass and, with so much green in front of him, he lifted his shoulders and began running hard. Suddenly, two defenders smacked him from opposite directions. Bubba fumbled the ball and Central Florida recovered—Tulane turnover No. 2. Up in the stands, Patti felt as if she'd been hit just as hard as her son.

Just two plays later, UCF running back Jason Peters galloped 50 yards for a touchdown.

Central Florida recovered the lead, 20-14, with 4:40 left in the half. Ricard again marched Tulane downfield. When they were 10 yards from the end zone, Ricard lobbed a pass toward its left corner, where three UCF defenders happened to be. Just as Patti felt like there was no way Tulane could mess this up, there was the third Tulane turnover. Cornerback Joe Burnett tipped Ricard's pass and linebacker Ronnell Sandy caught it at the goal line.

It wasn't just Patti cringing in the stands. Shaun King, the NFL quarterback and former Tulane star, suffered as well. King, an Orlando native, had come to support his old team.

Central Florida would score one more time that half, again thanks to a Tulane miscue. Tulane cornerback Bruce Youmans, a senior, committed pass interference on a third down. Three plays later, the Golden Knights scored a touchdown with only seven seconds left in the half, giving them a 27-14 lead.

The second half began differently. Ricard, who started the game with a lazy interception, started the second half with poise, throwing two third-down darts, the second a 49-yarder to Brown. But once inside the red zone, the offense became stuck in the mud and had to settle for a Jacob Hartgroves field goal.

UCF responded with a touchdown pass, thrown by the dynamic running back Smith, making it 34-17, UCF. Tulane's offense then sputtered. With the ball back, UCF went to ground control, the drive spilling into the fourth quarter. The Golden Knights ran the ball on 12 of 17 plays, but the final play was a missed field goal.

Richard came back and promptly marched Tulane 61 yards for a touchdown, surprising everyone. Each time Ricard stepped on the field, no one knew which quarterback would set up behind center. It had been like this all year. At times, he looked like an NFL prospect. Other times, he looked more like fourth-stringer Dawson. And the inconsistency wasn't game to game; it was drive to drive. On this ominous night, with Tulane down 10 with 5:16 left, Ricard would have two more drives to save the season from a downward spiral.

Thanks to mammoth tackles by Cannon and Spincer, Tulane's defense forced a punt with 3:34 left. After gaining a first down, Ricard stepped back in the pocket, five receivers darting downfield. Four were in single coverage. Three had open space between themselves and their defender. Brown, though, had two men covering him, one in front of him and one behind him. Despite the coverage, Ricard picked Brown. The pass hit a linebacker on the back—which in and of itself is appalling—and careened into the hands of Burdett, the cornerback who had tipped Ricard's previous interception. Burdett shuffled through the fuming Tulane offensive linemen until Parenton toppled him: Tulane turnover No. 4.

But Cannon and Spincer, the proud senior linebackers, weren't going to allow one astonishingly awful pass ruin their chance at a win. Again, each made a key stop. Again, UCF couldn't convert on third down. With 2:09 left and from the Tulane 28, UCF missed a field goal attempt.

This was it; there was no margin for error, and Ricard would have to move fast. He stood behind center and punctured the defense with short passes while the clock seemed frozen. Ricard's third completion was identical to the pass Terranova had fumbled earlier in the night. This time, Bubba held onto the football as his mother held her breath. Another first down. Ricard, with the moxie of a Shaun King or a J.P. Losman, completed two more. Suddenly there was 1:19 left in the game, with the ball on the UCF 15 and the few Tulane fans in the bleachers sitting on pins and needles.

Three receivers got into their stances to Ricard's left, two more two his right. Ricard caught the snap in his regular shotgun formation, took two steps back, one in place, and then stepped forward, his eyes fixated the entire time on the back left corner of the end zone. The receiver Guidroz, who began his route on the left hash mark on the 15, curved left toward the end zone near the 2-yard line and slowed his stride as he diagonally crossed the goal line, planning to time his jump. Ricard's spiral was headed straight for the back left pylon. Guidroz had timed it right. The receiver leapt into the air.

But so did cornerback Burnett, who slipped in front of Guidroz and made an acrobatic interception in the end zone: Tulane turnover No. 5. The game was over, the final score 34-24, UCF.

Tulane had lost a heartbreaker to Mississippi State, blown the second half to Houston, played soft against UTEP, and beat a Division I-AA opponent by just one touchdown. But no postgame locker room had the despair, not to mention the raw anger and embarrassment, of the locker room after the five-turnover UCF loss. Cannon, who again led Tulane in tackles, just sat in his locker chair, still in his complete uniform, his eyes darting at various teammates.

Just then, Shaun King suddenly burst into the room. He was the closest thing Tulane football had to a legend. In 1998, the record-breaking quarterback had run the explosive offense, leading Tulane to a magical 12-0 season. Beginning in 2006, one non-BCS team would annually earn a bid into a BCS Bowl. But back in 1998, undefeated Tulane played in the Liberty Bowl, beating Brigham Young. It was King's last game at Tulane, and Coach Scelfo's first. He had replaced Tommy Bowden, who left Tulane for Clemson after the undefeated regular season. After Tulane's bowl victory, King was drafted in the second round by the Tampa Bay Buccaneers, and as a rookie found himself starting the NFC Championship Game. By 2005, he was an NFL backup, and remained a proud Tulane alum.

Following the UCF loss, Coach Scelfo allowed King into the locker room. What happened next resonated throughout the locker room and the rest of the season.

King started his impromptu speech by talking about the old days, about Tulane's offensive dominance. He talked about pride, how his teams had defined the word. And then, he locked eyes with Ricard. King suddenly erupted. His speech turned into a tirade. He screamed about the trend of great quarterbacks at Tulane, and questioned Ricard's respect for the position. Ricard finished the night 27-for-47 for 260 yards and three touchdowns. Those numbers were pretty good. But they were dwarfed, essentially erased, by the four interceptions, two of them in the end zone. In the locker room Ricard sat in his chair, head down.

"You could see the tears coming from Shaun's face as he was yelling at us," said Parenton, Ricard's best friend. "You could tell he cared a lot about Tulane. And that was the distinguishing characteristic of the 12-0 team—they bled green and were proud to be part of Tulane.

"I took something positive from that speech. It made you feel good in a weird way, because he said nothing good about us, but it was awesome. It was much needed. . . . He basically said, Check your manhood."

The players, one by one, slowly walked onto the busses, headed for the Orlando airport. As the busses rolled away from the stadium and Wilma's early winds whipped rain around Orlando, a paltry group of Tulane fans stood on the sidewalk. They held handmade signs and cheered in high-pitched chirps, seemingly oblivious to the rain and to the loss.

"We could not leave the stadium until we saw those busses pull away," Patti Terranova said. "We needed them to know we were in total support of everything they did. And that we believed in them."

Though they were few in numbers and drenched by the rains, the Tulane fans stood there proud, supportive, and committed. Shaun King, had he seen their efforts, would have been proud of them.

CHAPTER 15

Home

$\mathcal{I}$n a normal football season, Tulane assistants would travel throughout the south on Thursdays, scouting and recruiting high school students. Then, on Saturday, the assistants would meet Tulane wherever the game was being held that weekend. In 2005, recruiting efforts were shaved; instead, coaches spent the time scouting out their own homes.

At different points during the season, Scelfo allowed coaches and players to return to New Orleans and visit. On one of these visits, Tulane assistant coach Garret Chachere (pronounced "Sasher-ay") returned to his home in Gentilly, a neighborhood just northeast of the French Quarter. At first, he wasn't granted access into his neighborhood. On every main avenue he tried, a National Guardsman would tell him that civilians weren't allowed. Even after pleading with them and explaining the situation—all he wanted to do was see his house, see how badly it had been damaged—he'd be turned away. Finally, a guardsman from a Missouri unit let him through.

Chachere drove the wrong way on one-way streets to save time. His was the only car on the road. Earlier in September, a friend had told Chachere that he'd driven a boat down Chachere's street. Now, in some parts of the area, Chachere couldn't even see the street because it was covered in tree limbs and other debris. He eventually found and drove down the street he lived on. Stop signs had fallen and traffic lights were still not functioning. Home after home on his block had been smashed, reduced to just their shells. He searched for something that was still intact, something to remind him of the neighborhood before the storm. He then spotted his backyard deck, where his kids used to play in the afternoon sun. The deck was in another home's frontyard. It had floated there.

He finally arrived at his own home. The yard was filled with trash and items that didn't belong to him. He deduced that his belongings, like his deck, must also now be in someone else's yard. He approached his front door, keys in hand. He pushed and kicked, but the door wouldn't budge; the floodwaters had swollen it shut. Not knowing what else he could do, he walked back to his car, figuring he'd try his parents' home, which was also in the neighborhood.

As he drove down the desecrated streets, he approached his parents' home, the house where he was raised. He thought about how hard his parents had worked to build that home, how much love and money they'd poured into it, how it was still a symbol of his childhood. All these thoughts came to a halt when he saw the house; it had been completely destroyed. He stopped his car and just stared at it, unable to speak. He thought of his parents having to deal with this utter devastation. And he thought of all the other people who had devoted decades to making this city the eclectic and proud place it was. He thought about how long it would take to rebuild, and whether or not rebuilding would even be feasible or worthwhile. He worried that Katrina had smothered the soul of this place. He began to cry.

○ ○ ○

Many players were just as desperate to see their homes, especially after Chachere described what he'd seen on his visit. Brandon Spincer decided it was time for him to make the trip. He and five teammates obtained a pass into the city from the coach, then loaded in a truck and headed to New Orleans, anxious to see what Katrina had left behind. The highway was empty. Their truck drove down Interstate 10, past an abandoned boat. For Spincer, images like this just wouldn't sink in; he couldn't believe this was New Orleans.

They took the looping exit onto Claiborne Avenue, a few miles from Tulane. As the car spilled onto Claiborne, the only cars they saw were those stacked on top of others. Popular fast food restaurants looked like they had caught on fire. Roofs sat next to buildings. There was no sign of life until they approached the major intersection at Napoleon Avenue, where Spincer spotted an Army truck. Soldiers manned the streets with M-16s just a few yards from the home of Anthony Cannon and Sean Lucas.

Cannon and Lucas were not just roommates; they'd been best friends for over a decade. They were the kind of friends who could finish each other's sentences. From backyard ball to high school stardom, they had always been teammates, too.

They even ran on the same 400-meter relay team at Stephenson (Georgia) High, and their squad won the overall state championship. Together, they left the Atlanta area for New Orleans in August of 2002. By September, they were making the Saturday night news. Lucas was a speedy Tulane cornerback, who, by 2005, would evolve into a defensive-savvy safety. Cannon was a textbook linebacker, the type of snarling, ferocious player coaches found only once every few years. Cannon led Tulane in tackles in every season he played. He won the team's off-season weight-room award, earning the nickname "The Incredible Hulk."

The pair was adopted by New Orleans thanks in part to their success on the football field. The roommates were inseparable, be it in the locker room or at the campus food court. "Sean," Cannon sighed, "is like my wife." First, they roomed in the dorms, and then they moved into an apartment in Uptown on Napoleon and Claiborne. They lived right across the street from a Walgreens. That first night at the Dallas Doubletree, they had both spotted the store, surrounded by floodwaters, on CNN.

Now, smashed dining room tables and broken washing machines sat outside Lucas and Cannon's home. The street was a graveyard of houses. Floodwater had made its way to the tops of the roofs. Even though the Tulane seniors knew from the television image that their home had been flooded, there was that glimmer of hope, of implausibility, that maybe theirs had been spared.

Lucas walked inside and slowly pulled out his cell phone. "Hey, man," he told his best friend. "It's gone." Cannon remained calm on the other end. He was back in Ruston, helpless.

Home

The week before his freshman season, Lucas' home in Georgia had burned to the ground. He'd lost everything. Years later, he stood in his New Orleans home, taking in a second loss. This time he was able to salvage something: his Hawaii Bowl ring.

o o o

It was time for Spincer to see his parents' house; he'd lived with them until January of 2004. He drove down his street thinking that it looked like a bomb had been dropped. He slowly walked out of the car and toward the front door, which was surrounded by smashed windows. He looked at the doorknob for a few seconds, debating whether or not to turn it, thinking to himself that if he didn't open the door then he wouldn't have to deal with what was inside. If Spincer's neighborhood looked this bad from the outside, he couldn't imagine what would be behind the door. He placed his key in the lock and turned the knob. He took a breath and braced himself.

Everything was in its place. He squinted at the walls, looking for a water line. There wasn't one. A large tree had fallen in the backyard, but had missed the house. God, Spincer was convinced, had a hand in all of this. He whipped out his cell phone and called his mother, Barbara, in Greenville, Mississippi. "Everything's fine!" he said.

"Everything?" she said in disbelief. He reassured her: "Everything." His mother asked him to grab her Tulane jersey. During the evacuation frenzy, she had forgotten to pack it. She wanted to wear it on November's Senior Day, when she and Spincer's father would greet the linebacker on the field in a pregame ceremony.

He rejoined his teammates in the truck and they toured their homes. Spincer's apartment was also spared. Same for cornerback Jeremy Foreman. But Mason and Darren Sapp lived off the Interstate 10 Service Road. There, the white sofa inside was now green. Four feet of water had inundated their home. And the home of Youmans and Boger was now a greenhouse of mold. The only things Youmans could salvage were some shoes.

For Spincer, he felt blessed that his homes were salvageable, but that was a fleeting blessing. The city he cherished had been battered. And his neighbors and classmates from St. Augustine hadn't all had the same luck. "It's one thing when you know a couple people displaced," Lucas said of Spincer's hometown. "But for him, it's the majority of people he knows."

As the season progressed, dozens of players discovered their apartments were also destroyed. Sometimes in Ruston, a person could tell which player had just returned from New Orleans by the look on the player's face. Weeks after Lucas called Cannon with the news that their apartment had been destroyed, Cannon made the trip down for the clean up.

Cannon placed bags over his feet. Then he put on thick gloves and placed a mask over his mouth. The seemingly fearless linebacker was afraid to enter his own home. He stepped through the front door. The first thing that hit him was the odor. He thought to himself, *This smell is worse than vomit.*

Part of him wished the storm had just washed everything away. Then he wouldn't have had to see his belongings in their ruined state. Instead, everything awaited him inside. When he got to his bedroom, he peeked in slowly. He entered and stayed for only a minute. His bed was still made, except it was painted with green and black mold splotches. Once sturdy desktops were concave and feeble. Clothing, splattered with mold, hung on a slanted rack in the closest. There was his letterman's jacket, its significance diminished beneath the lather of grime. Game tapes from previous seasons were ruined.

On top of the television sat Cannon's trophy, awarded for his weightlifting triumphs. The trophy looked like it had melted.

Cannon trudged through the hallway and out their front door. While he drove down Napoleon Avenue, he gazed out the window. "Houses that I usually see every day, full of life, were pretty much dead," Cannon said. "The whole city was dead to me."

○ ○ ○

On his second trip to his home in the Gentilly neighborhood, Chachere called in a favor. He arranged for a New Orleans police escort to drive Chachere and his wife, Lauren, to their house. When they reached the front door, the cop handed Chachere his gun. The cop explained he could possibly lose his job if he shot someone in Chachere's home, but in the first weeks after Hurricane Katrina, he sure as hell wasn't going to let the coach go in his home without safety; this time, they'd found the once-stuck front door wide open.

In the two weeks since Chachere's first visit, government authorities had gone by every house in Gentilly, smashed through the doors, and searched inside for signs of life. But there was no way to know if anyone would now be inside. Looting had been rampant in the neighborhood, and there was also the chance that there could be wild animals inside.

Chachere stood on his doorstep, holding a gun for the first time in his life. The lights were out. Sun slipped in through the windows, creating maddening shadows. Faint creaking sounds gave him shivers as he gripped the gun. Chachere didn't know what he was doing, so he emulated cops he'd seen on television, taking slow, patient steps. From afar, he heard his wife tell the cop, "He doesn't know how to shoot a gun. He's not going to shoot anybody." But Chachere thought to himself, *I would shoot somebody today.*

"Is anybody here?" the football coach screamed nervously. He thought to himself that if anything moved, it was getting shot. He might not hit it, but it was getting shot at. There would be no hesitating, no second-guessing. He was standing in his front hallway, near the stairs to his children's rooms, afraid. "Is anybody here?" Chachere screamed again. He heard nothing.

Only then, after he had vowed to shoot an intruder, did Chachere take a deep breath and comprehend his surroundings. He was inside his home. The water line was eight feet high.

Couches were where tables had been. Tables were where couches had been. He became numb, thinking to himself that this was all a nightmare, and he would wake up and tell Lauren how outrageous the dream was.

The Chacheres wandered aimlessly around their first floor, their eyes watering from the smell and the sadness. After five minutes, they went outside to regroup. The Chacheres had arrived in a rented truck. Their plan—if they could get inside the house—had been to gather as much of their life as possible and load up the truck before sundown. So they put masks over their mouths and got to work, picking up the pieces of their life from a soggy floor. They couldn't get into one of the rooms because the entertainment center had fallen, blocking the entrance. Their home was coated in mold, dust, and muck. They were afraid to lift anything too heavy; if one of them got injured, they were helpless. No hospitals in the area were open.

They collected the old baby clothes of six-year-old Grant and three-year-old Noah. They took pictures from the walls and off the mantel; some of the pictures of grandmothers and great-grandmothers had been ruined. But they took them anyway.

The downstairs area was a complete disaster, but what they found upstairs was a different story. The second floor was untouched and neat, exactly the way they left it just before evacuating. The stark contrast displayed itself again and again as they walked up and down the stairs: what was and what is, past and present, memory and reality. Over six hours, they packed up what was left, loaded it into their truck, and drove away, the sun setting in the background.

CHAPTER 16

Winning

The first practice after the disheartening loss to Central Florida happened on Tuesday, October 25. On that afternoon, Scelfo ran a popular drill that involved both offensive and defensive lineman. One member from each side would face the other, just like they did in the trenches on Saturdays. When a coach blew the whistle, the two players would explode from their stances and violently attack each other until the weaker one was thrown to the side. Scelfo had every player except punters and kickers participate in the drill. Players were matched up with teammates by size, and when they heard the whistle, a line of battles took place: pads pounding, helmets clanking, players howling.

With the intensity of a general, Scelfo marched from skirmish to skirmish, sticking his head in close to the dangerous action. "Move your feet!" he screamed at left tackles and quarterbacks alike. Finally, after each player had participated in at least one of these battles, Scelfo brought his team into a large huddle. In a booming voice, he yelled, "We had it! We lost it! I want it back! We have to be physical, and we have to get that attitude back. Get it back!"

Scelfo wasn't in denial; he knew getting "it" back could be physically impossible, especially if "it" had been left behind in August. He knew very well that winning a football game would be difficult for this team. But he was going to teach lessons about perseverance, regardless of the scoreboard or the team's record. He had to keep lighting fires. He was going to control the things he could control, so he would continue to ignite his team. He saw it as his responsibility to dig into these players and find their pride. His boys, he determined, were going to look back at 2005 and think, *We may have lost games, but in the end, I won because I learned that I was strong.*

Understandably, there were some doubters on the team. The weekdays were tough enough on the players, who dealt with displacement, homesickness, and hurricane stress. Add to that the losses on Saturdays, and some of them began to see their losing record as a late hit on an already sacked quarterback. It was hard for them to believe that through all the losing, they were actually winning. But Scelfo was trying to teach his team to approach each day as a singular battle. Don't think back to the Central Florida loss, he told them. And don't try to win the next five games this afternoon at practice. Instead, become a smarter, stronger player, and a smarter, stronger person, *today.* Striving daily toward this goal would only benefit the team, regardless of what the scoreboard said.

From a coaching standpoint, it was sometimes difficult to teach perseverance while doubting one's own toughness. Teaching a nickel package sometimes didn't have the same importance as it normally would have when placed against the thought of your deck floating away into someone else's yard. More trying on the coaching staff's focus was the fact that many of them were separated from their families. For instance, offensive line coach Don Mahoney's wife and children were in Michigan. He'd missed his son's first day of kindergarten. He was sad every day, but he never let it show up on the practice field, instead focusing his paternal energy on his linemen—his sons for the season. Even those coaches who did have their families with them in Ruston suffered, knowing they were homeless in New Orleans. But Scelfo had daily talks with his assistants, encouraging them to go on just as he did his players. Scelfo's staff continued to teach with passion, study film with enthusiasm, and coach effectively—all of it with the belief that a win on the field was still very much within Tulane's reach.

On October 29, the team traveled to Mobile, Alabama. The folks there offered Tulane access to Ladd-Peebles Stadium, fittingly colored in green and white, so that the Green Wave held its home game there against Marshall. In a season where every game would be played in a different city, this was their fifth of six "home" games, the others happening in Shreveport, Baton Rouge, Lafayette, and Ruston.

The evening had all the ingredients of a typical 2005 Tulane game: the opponent scored easily on its first drive; Tulane's running backs couldn't move the ball; Ricard was yanked for a backup. Still, there was a little magic that night. In the previous three games, Tulane hadn't caused a turnover, but had committed nine. In the second quarter against Marshall, with the Green Wave down 7-0, Tulane's Youmans dashed in front of a receiver, snatched the pass from mid-air, and ran 51 yards, untouched, for a touchdown. Then Ricard, back on the field after having been benched, threw a perfectly timed pass to Preston Brown for a 34-yard touchdown. A blocked kick, though, kept the score 13-7. But then Jovon Jackson notched a rushing touchdown late in the first half, which was followed by the Tulane defense causing a second turnover. Perhaps the intense practices had paid off. All week, Scelfo's voice had resonated through helmets. He'd said that the defense would lose the game if they didn't create turnovers, and now here they were, rising to the challenge made by their fiery coach.

Down 20-7, Marshall came out of the locker room energized. Chubb Small, the aptly named 5-foot-9 kick returner for Marshall, ran back the third-quarter kickoff 92 yards for a touchdown. As the game went on, nothing seemed to work offensively for Tulane. Ricard's efforts that night were paltry, totaling just 97 yards. Coach Scelfo tried subbing in seldom-used backup Nick Cannon (no relation to the linebacker Anthony), but that didn't seem to spark Ricard's desire to play better. Late in the third quarter, Tulane's Chris Beckman had already booted seven punts.

With 2:11 left in the third, Marshall lobbed a deep pass. Boger, Tulane's safety net, was the last man back, and he grabbed the ball with ease on his 35. Boger sprinted toward the left sideline. At the Marshall 45, he cut right, and 11 Marshall players simultaneously locked their cleats in the grass. Boger ran diagonally toward the right corner of the end zone, Marshall's offensive linemen pathetically huffing behind him. Their quarterback, Brian Skinner, was the only player even in reach of Boger, and Lucas, blocking for his fellow senior, put his hands on Skinner, stalling him long enough for Boger to cross the goal line. Ricard's two-point conversion pass failed, but Tulane led 26-14 heading into the fourth quarter.

It seemed impossible for any team with this much momentum to blow a must-win game like this one. But despite Tulane's smiles on the sidelines, Marshall began to wake up. They scored a touchdown with 8:38 left, and on the ensuing possession, Ricard threw an interception. Marshall was well aware of Tulane's fourth-quarter fatigue, and they took full advantage of it. Nine of the 10 plays on the next drive were runs, and running back Ahmad Bradshaw scored with 2:10 left, Marshall's first lead since the first quarter. Marshall logically went for two, but, sure enough, couldn't convert a rush. Still, they were leading 27-26.

Just like in the previous week's game at Central Florida, Tulane trailed in the fourth but had possession late and was still in contention. The game came down to a fourth-and-5 with 1:25 left. A pass intended for Brown left Ricard's hand, sailed into the Alabama sky, and was batted away by Marshall's Chris Royal. It was another loss, one far too similar to the previous week's against UCF.

"There was no way we should have lost that game," said Brandon Spincer. "We were trying to persevere and remain focused, and we thought we were doing a great job, but we were not getting the results." Tulane, now 2-5, hadn't tasted victory in a month—and the victory against Division-II SLU had been bittersweet, barely a victory at all. "What do we have to do to get another win?" Spincer said.

Tulane arrived at the Mobile airport after the Marshall loss around midnight. Their charter plane was not there, further convincing the team that nothing could go right. But there in that airport, the players took a deep breath. Many realized that no matter how frustrated they were—mostly the defense at the offense—all they had was each other. They began talking and relaxing, remembering that come Monday they were all students trying to maneuver around an unfamiliar campus. They remembered that they needed each other. As these bonds healed, Coach Scelfo fell asleep in an airport chair next to his daughter.

○ ○ ○

Mathematically, at 2-5, Tulane needed to win every ball game left to make a bowl game. Their next game, against Navy, did not start out in a way that reaffirmed their hopes.

Playing in front of a raucous home crowd in Annapolis, Maryland, Navy scampered to a touchdown on its first possession. Route fumbled the kickoff return, and five plays later, Navy doubled the score. Then Ricard threw an interception. Navy scored on the ensuing drive. Ricard then threw another interception, and again, Navy scored on the ensuing drive. With 3:42 left in the first quarter, Navy led 28-0.

In the second quarter, Scelfo replaced Ricard with backup Scott Elliott. Navy took a 35-0 lead before Tulane finally scored, with 40 seconds left in the first half. When it was over, Navy had 418 rushing yards. Tulane lost, 49-21, and was officially bowl ineligible.

Toward the end of the sixth loss, Bubba Terranova, who'd always been his mother's shoulder to cry on, began to have tears in his own eyes. He squinted through the blur at his fellow seniors, who shared a feeling of despair to which the younger players on the team were oblivious. This group of seniors had been a part of the Hawaii Bowl team in 2002, and they understood the pure satisfaction of playing in a bowl, the validation of earning an extra game. They hadn't dismissed the effects of their perseverance so far in 2005, but they'd always believed that their strength after Katrina would translate into victories on Saturdays.

For some players, the disappointment turned to rage. Anthony Cannon found himself furious with his teammates because they hadn't risen to his level of play. He was arguably the best linebacker in Conference USA and was among the country's leaders in tackles, but there was only so much he could do on his own. He was a passionate leader on the defense and was admired by everyone on the team, but he also had a short temper. His quick fuse sometimes ignited his play during games, but it had also caused problems around campus, like when, earlier in the season, he'd thrown his helmet at Mendow, the equipment manager.

Although Cannon was a strong person, he, like many of his teammates, was dealing with the loss of his home and other hurricane trauma. Those emotions, in combination with his temper, made for a volatile recipe, and after his team became ineligible for a bowl, the rage spilled out. The week after the sixth loss, as the team prepared for its game against the Rice Owls, Cannon cracked during a defensive drill, yelling back at Coach Chachere. The two men began screaming at each other, and Cannon slammed his helmet into the ground. Coach Scelfo, on the other end of the field, walked over and spoke to Cannon privately. What he told the star linebacker was simple: he was done for the week. For the first time in four years, Cannon would not play in a game.

Coach Scelfo was well aware that his team was on edge, and if a player got away with this type of misbehavior, it could open the door to more defiance. Scelfo had poured too much energy into molding this team to let one incident unravel it. It didn't matter that Cannon was the best player. No player was bigger than a coach, and no coach was bigger than the team.

The next game would be played in Houston at Rice University. The Owls held the nation's longest losing streak—14 games. Coach Scelfo decided to shake things up and start freshman Jordan Ellis in Cannon's position. He also decided to start freshman Scott Elliot at quarterback. In the second half against Navy, Elliott hadn't played that badly; he'd finished 13-for-26 for 109 yards. The game against Rice would be the first college start for both Elliott and Ellis.

All season long, Ellis had faced a firing squad of misfortune. His home in Pass Christian, Mississippi had been destroyed. He was losing pounds by the dozens. Then, the Wednesday before the October UTEP game, he'd suffered a staph infection, battling a 103-fever while losing feeling in one leg. He had been rushed to the hospital. The next day, he'd undergone surgery on the back of his calf. He attended the UTEP game but didn't dress in uniform. He couldn't practice the next week, and didn't make the trip to Central Florida. The team was the one thing that prevented him from overwhelming emptiness, but by then, he didn't even feel like he was part it. He became depressed, just as he had been those nights at the Dallas Doubletree. Finally, he was cleared to play, and did so on special teams against Marshall. He'd done the same in the Navy game. Now, against Rice, he was suddenly a starter.

Before the Rice game, in a rickety old locker room, Brandon Spincer stood to speak. He stared into his teammates' faces, into their vacant eyes, and sensed a frightening complacency just minutes before kickoff; they looked ready to lose. They needed a jolt, he thought, so he explained that, yes, their chance at a bowl game was gone, but not their pride. No one could take that away from them.

Scott Elliott, a Texas native, jogged onto the field, which happened to be the same field where he made his first start in high school. His opening drive as a college starter led to a field goal. It was the first time Tulane scored on its opening drive since the SLU game over a month before.

The defense came onto the field for the first time in the game. Spincer peered into the stands. His two children had spent the fall with their mother in Houston, and this was the first time he'd seen them since Hurricane Katrina. It was also Brandon Jr.'s first Tulane football game. Once Spincer spotted his children in the stands, he made sure to look up at them after every play he made.

The game was a whirlwind of offense thanks to Tulane's wildcat freshman quarterback and Rice's multifaceted option offense. During the game, Cannon arrived on the sideline. He had driven five hours by himself from Ruston to Houston. He quietly approached Coach Scelfo during the game and asked if he could put on a uniform and play. Without question, Tulane could have used Cannon that day. But Scelfo could not give in, could not compromise his beliefs. He was making a point to the team, and no multifaceted option offense could make Scelfo go back on his word.

Scelfo was ready to play Ricard at quarterback if Elliott ever stalled, but the Texan was firing all afternoon. He finished 22-for-37 for 298 yards and three touchdowns, despite a wobbly ball dubbed by his coach as the "ugliest ball in America."

With both offenses playing well—Rice accumulated 506 total yards of offense—the score seesawed all day, with eight lead changes in all. With 4:48 left in the game, Rice scored its sixth touchdown, and first from a pass, and the Owls expanded their lead to 42-34. Tulane couldn't rally one last swing. And, just like that, the game was over, and Tulane had lost.

As the players lumbered off the field, Spincer's children waited for him outside the locker room. He mustered a smile. He kissed his daughter and picked up his son, carrying him into the locker room. Spincer, in his tattered uniform, sat on one knee while Brandon Jr., wearing a bright yellow shirt, stood in front of his father.

Coach Scelfo stood before his players and told them he was not disappointed. They had played their hearts out. They had bounced back from the embarrassment at Navy and—just as Spincer had demanded in his pregame pep talk—played with obvious pride. Spincer made 10 tackles that day, a team best. On a day when pride reigned, he looked down at his son and smiled; all those lonely nights in Ruston, and all those days of study and practice, came into focus.

After his speech, Scelfo spotted Cannon outside the locker room. The coach put his arm around the player. Scelfo looked into Cannon's embarrassed eyes and told him the truth: that Cannon cost the team the game by not playing. Cannon averaged 10.2 tackles per game; that day, Ellis had made four. But Scelfo also told him that for the rest of his life, he had to put things in perspective, understand what was at stake, and understand being part of a team. For Cannon, too, everything came into focus.

Tulane had played hard against Rice, but once again, there was no Victory Sunday. By Tuesday, reality had settled in; Tulane did not have the fuel to win a game. And this time, they had lost to a winless team. The team had already started to feel that things might have to get worse before they got better—a thought they'd pushed out of their minds each week. But with each loss—even the ones that were hard fought—ignoring that feeling became harder and harder to do.

CHAPTER 17

Support

erranova looked at his buzzing cell phone. Barrett Pepper normally never called him this early.

"Bubba," the Tulane kicker said that Sunday after the Rice game. "Did you hear about Beckman? He got shot." Chris Beckman, the punter, was one of Terranova's closest friends on the team.

"Come on, man. That's not funny," Terranova said.

"I'm serious."

Terranova hung up and hustled from the campus cafeteria up to Pepper's dorm room. There sat Pepper, fellow kicker Michael Sager, and deep snapper Craig Gelhardt. All were stone-faced. They told him Beckman was in the Intensive Care Unit.

"I felt the worst pain," Terranova said later of the moment. "The hurricane had nothing on that."

○ ○ ○

Back when Beckman was a student at Grenada (Mississippi) High, some teammates invited him out one night. These guys were country boys, campus stars, and know-it-alls at age 17. Beckman played the part, with his Mississippi accent and ball field success. His teammates started bragging about what they had done earlier: driven aimlessly around town, smashing mailboxes with baseball bats. Beckman looked at these boys and their grins. He thought for a moment and calmly said, "C'mon guys, that's stupid." And they didn't do it again. It was stories like these—more than his brilliant punts—that made Chris' father, Bob Beckman, proud.

Chris Beckman was a genuinely nice guy. He was honest and as wholesome as the Mississippi town in which he was raised. In his bedroom back in Grenada, five hours from New Orleans, his father loved to show the photo of Beckman when Beckman was "leetle-beetee," draped in camouflage, deer hunting at age 11, hoisting a 7-point. Some boys decorate their bedrooms with baseball or football items; Beckman's bedroom was splattered with hunting memorabilia. There were framed pictures of mallards; guns; a closest filled with more than 10 camouflage jackets; stuffed ducks that Beckman had shot during hunting seasons.

He could kill a deer, but he would run from a bee. His older brother, Daniel, used to tease him about it. One day, Chris was mowing the lawn, and he suddenly started sprinting in circles, trying to avoid a buzzing bee. Another time, the family was on a highway during a road trip, and Beckman spotted a road sign. "See, I told y'all!" he said. "They even got killer bees up here." The sign indeed had an illustration of a bee. It told passersby: "Bee Alert."

Beckman became the first Grenada student since the 1980s to play Division I-A football. He showed up at Tulane, where many of the students hail from the northeast, with his guitar, his bike, and his camouflage trucker hat. In a French class, the professor asked how many of the students had been to Paris. Every student raised a hand, except Beckman. When he told this to his father, Bob said in his Mississippi drawl, "You should have asked how many of them know how to blow a duck-caller. You would have been the only one!"

Beckman, with his genuine charm and likable goofiness, became a team favorite among kickers and linebackers alike. He also became one of the better punters in Conference USA, leading all punters with a 42.6-yard average as a sophomore in 2004. After that season, Terranova moved in with his buddy Pepper. Terranova really didn't know much about Pepper's other roommate, the punter. But in the spring of 2005, Beckman and Terranova quickly became close friends. They would walk over to Tulane's recreation center and shoot pool for hours, continuously talking trash. Then they would go back home, tear open a case of Natural Light, and play a drinking game called quarters.

Occasionally during the days, Terranova would be in his room and he would hear a pinging sound. It was Beckman, practicing quarters. Those nights, when they ran out of beer, they would head over to a campus bar such as The Boot, where the effervescent punter picked up women like he was a Saints quarterback. "Now, he's not the cutest guy, not at all," Terranova said. "But his personality, he can make anybody laugh."

○ ○ ○

Beckman was sprawled on his back in the bed of a speeding pickup truck, pressing his hand on his abdomen, red blood seeping through his green Tulane T-shirt. The pain seized his entire body. His stomach was burning. He began tapping his heels incessantly. He peered up and saw the blur of green pine trees in the woods. His glossy-eyed brother knelt beside him. "Daniel," Beckman said, "I'm not going to die."

"Not today," his brother said.

Daniel, 32, had dreamed of one day going on an African safari. He saved money over the years, finally splurging on a .416 Rigby, a gun that his dad called "an elephant gun." The bullets for that gun, Bob Beckman said, were 410-grain solid bullets, which cost $180 for 20.

Early Sunday morning, the Beckman brothers and two of Daniel's friends had ventured into the woods, about five miles north of Ruston. They had cut a metal-plate target, but rounded the edges with a torch. They didn't realize that by using the torch, they had hardened the metal. One of the friends shot the elephant gun, the bullet clapping against the metal target. It ricocheted, which they hadn't anticipated. The bullet had zipped back and had struck Beckman in the abdomen.

At 9 a.m. later that morning, the phone rang in Pam and Bob Beckman's home. The first call only provided snippets: "Chris was shot in a hunting accident. We're headed to the hospital in Ruston. He is conscious." Bob tried desperately to calm his bawling wife, explaining that Beckman probably was shot with a 22-caliber bullet, which could kill, but wasn't as dangerous as, perhaps, a larger bullet. Moments later, Bob was on the phone with Daniel, and asked him if Chris was shot by a .22. There was silence on the other end.

"No, daddy, he got shot with a Rigby." Bob turned to his wife: "Pam, we got a problem." They loaded their Nissan Quest Van and headed toward Ruston.

When they arrived at Lincoln General Hospital, Daniel was waiting outside. So were Coach Scelfo and a few assistants. Inside, the 22-year-old Beckman was fighting for his life. While they waited for the surgeon to arrive from Monroe, a nurse accidentally ruptured blood vessels in his nose while trying to insert a tube. Soon, Beckman began gagging. Daniel rushed over, and Beckman vomited blood on his brother. The doctor, Jeb Butler, arrived and promptly filled Beckman with morphine, beginning life-saving surgery. The bullet had entered the liver, so the doctor determined it would make more sense to leave the bullet there for now than to cause more damage with removal. A four-inch incision was made in the middle of his chest.

Early Monday morning, the Beckmans were able to enter their son's room. His mother Pam, who worked as a nurse, began to scan the monitors with her teary eyes. In front of his family, Bob Beckman was a rock. His wife, understandably, was a mess, and Bob knew he had to harness his emotions in order to help Pam harness her own. But keeping up a strong façade was hard. Finally, Bob sneaked into a public bathroom at the hospital. He stared into a mirror and just asked, "Why?" Then, he began to sob.

Two days after being shot, the first thing Beckman muttered to his father was, "Daddy, don't blame Daniel."

o o o

Terranova hadn't slept that first night. His mind had wandered through the timeline of adversity that autumn. He asked himself, *What else could go wrong?* When Terranova finally got to the hospital, he first spotted Pam Beckman on her cell phone, crying. He thought of his own mother, who lived her life for her son.

On Tuesday, Terranova finally had the chance to speak to his dear friend. Beckman was breathing hard. It was surreal; his goofball friend, who was supposed to be cracking jokes and losing at drinking games, was in the hospital with a bullet in his liver.

Every day that week, Coach Scelfo sat in the waiting room. It was similar to those evacuation days when he sat in the Dallas Doubletree lobby, when football just didn't matter. He had taught his players the value of perseverance. Now they would have to redefine perseverance.

Scelfo had met Bob Beckman when Tulane recruited Chris. It was always a cordial relationship; both were good ol' boys who loved to crack jokes. But a month earlier, Bob had visited Ruston for a day and attended a practice. When Scelfo spotted him, the coach let down his guard, bypassing a cordial handshake for a bear hug. It was genuine reaction during a difficult time.

At the hospital, Scelfo sat next to Bob in the waiting room for hours at a time. He tried to get Bob's mind off of reality. They swapped old football stories, told an occasional joke. Scelfo looked at Bob and saw an ailing and needy father; he had seen this look on players' faces before. He thought, *This is what a coach does for a living, get folks through rough times.* This moment, like much of the 2005 season so far, was uncharted territory.

Back on campus, the team was solemn for the first 24 hours. They picked up tidbits of news, but didn't have specifics.

Tulane was scheduled to host Tulsa that Saturday in Monroe, Louisiana. "Up until we found out he would be all right," Spincer said, "the game didn't matter."

At 1:30 p.m. on Monday, Scelfo held a team meeting in the locker room. He stared at his football team with a serious face. First, he asked his team to say a prayer for their teammate. Then Scelfo began to give an impromptu sermon, telling his players that tomorrow is not promised. Sniffles were heard from the crowd. Terranova could not lift his head.

At practice, Terranova couldn't focus. Scelfo, preserving what little energy his troops had left, held light practices that week. The mood was sedated. There was loud coaching, but it wasn't angry. Scelfo held an open casting call for punters. Everyone from Pepper to the enormous tight end Jerome Landry gave it a shot. Scelfo chose Pepper to replace his close friend at kicker, a position he'd never played in college.

During the week, Scelfo reminded the team about its valiant effort at Rice: "You played for pride last week, why wouldn't you this week?" He occasionally brought up Beckman, but was careful not make this a win-one-for-Chris game, because he thought the players had enough on their minds, and putting that additional strain on them would have been in bad taste. Most often, Scelfo brought up the seniors. There were two games remaining: Saturday at "home" against Tulsa and then the following weekend at Southern Mississippi. The latter was the game originally scheduled for the first weekend after Katrina.

The Tulsa game, played a half-hour away in Monroe, would be Tulane's Senior Day. In college football, there are a four sacred moments in most players' careers: the day he signs; his first game; his first bowl game; and Senior Day. Spincer, lying on his dorm bed on Wednesday, spent the night reminiscing about his career. He was looking forward to Senior Day, in part because he'd had to work hard to earn that senior status. Every year, a couple of players became academically ineligible, and they would talk the talk, telling their teammates they would be back with a vengeance the next season, but instead they would disappear and become a memory from the freshman dorm. But Spincer, a proud son and a proud father, studied harder and returned to the team, and by his senior year, he'd become one of its most important leaders. "I feel blessed," he said. "I plan on being successful in life, and I think that I'm on the right track to do that."

The November 16 Senior Day game took place in Monroe's Malone Stadium. It was a cloudy afternoon. The seniors assembled in the tunnel behind the end zone while the rest of the team awaited them on the field. Also on the field were the families of those seniors about to be recognized. An announcer briefly stated the accomplishments each player made during his time with the team, and at the conclusion of his speech, the player would jog out from the tunnel. They were each given a bouquet of flowers, which the player then gave to their mother.

Spincer had attended his first Senior Day game back in 2001. He had seen dozens of players go through this ritual. They'd always seemed so much older than him, so grown up. Now it was his turn. As the announcer summarized Spincer's time at Tulane, his parents waited for him, wearing the jerseys he'd recovered from their home in New Orleans. Next to them stood Mary Kennedy, Spincer's grandmother, who had traveled from Greenville, Mississippi, for Senior Day. He hadn't seen her since before Hurricane Katrina. He ran out on the field and joined them.

Senior Day gave every senior player—from Chris McGee, the left tackle from Beaumont, Texas, to Boger, Youmans, Dawson, and Mason—their moment of recognition. Cannon and Lucas got their chance to run out on the field. Of course, so did Bubba Terranova. "I was expecting to have to wear rain boots," joked Bubba, knowing Patti and her tears would be waiting for him out on the field.

Patti had been planning this day in her head for four years. Of course, she'd imagined it happening at the Superdome, and she'd imagined that every relative would be there. She'd always pictured a huge group waiting for Bubba on the field: her daughter, Bubba's grandparents, her brother and his wife. She'd pictured all of Bubba's friends from Salmen High waving to him from the stands. She'd pictured a packed stadium filled with Tulane fans and green jerseys. She'd rehearsed in her head how Senior Day would go, and had occasionally told her son, "Boy, you better hug me first!"

But this wasn't the Superdome; this was five hours away from home, which meant that most of Bubba's family hadn't made it, and neither had most of Tulane's fans. The announced crowd was 10,306. Clumps of fans were scattered around the stadium, dotting the bleachers. Patti stood on the field alone, the only one there to hug Bubba.

Although Terranova had predicted needing galoshes to protect him from his mother's tears, it was Coach Chachere who ended up needing tissues. He stood there and watched these men, many whom he'd recruited and coached, take the spotlight on a memorable day. He felt a raw pain for the seniors he had groomed and befriended; no other group had had as challenging a season and yet so meager a Senior Day. Chachere couldn't blame Tulane's fan base, but he still wished the event had been more like what he knew players and their families had been expecting since their very first game.

The team took the field that day with a decal on the back on their helmets: Beckman's No. 45. Sitting alone in the stands wearing a green Tulane jacket was Bob Beckman. Chris had wanted to be there, and though he was already out of the hospital, his doctor didn't want him outdoors. So his father represented them both. Bob had seen how the team rallied around his son, how the coach disregarded football to sit in the waiting room, how Terranova loved his teammate like a brother. He wanted to be at the game to support the team that had supported him after his son's accident.

On the opening kickoff, Scelfo tried to catch Tulsa off guard. The Green Wave attempted an onside kick, but Tulsa recovered the tricky bounce. On Tulsa's very first play, quarterback Paul Smith threw a 48-yard touchdown pass to Ashlan Davis. When Tulane got the ball back, Elliott actually responded with a touchdown drive, 13 plays, 76 yards. But Tulane wouldn't score again until the fourth quarter, and by that point, bowl-bound Tulsa had 38 points.

During the game, Patti Terranova had spotted Bob. They only knew each other through their sons, but that week's events had shown how close they'd all become. Channeling her son on the field, Patti hugged Bob, and Bob hugged back, each supporting the other.

CHAPTER 18

Thanksgiving

$\mathcal{T}$ulane's regular season was supposed to have ended by Thanksgiving 2005. Instead, Tulane had one more game: the original season opener against Southern Mississippi, which had been rescheduled for two days after Thanksgiving. If there were ever a year when Tulane players wanted to be home to give thanks with their families, it was this one. But instead, the team was in Ruston, preparing for the upcoming game and spending the holiday together.

After a light Thursday practice, Scelfo brought the team together and spoke from his heart. He told his players that he was thankful for having them as his team, regardless of their record. There was no other team with which he would have rather gone through the season. No other team would have had the character to endure what they'd been through.

Until that morning's practice, Antonio Mason hadn't even realized it *was* Thanksgiving. It was just another regular day in an irregular season. Sitting near his fellow senior linebackers, he talked about how he normally spent the holiday with family. In a way, he said, he was still doing just that, because the team had been the only family he'd had in the past few months.

Tulane's Thanksgiving dinner was actually brunch, a buffet inside the corridor of the Tech basketball arena. Brunch featured smoked turkey, green beans, cranberries, and pumpkin pie. The waft reminded players of home. One by one, they loaded their paper plates. Between bites, Mason said to the players sitting near him, "I am thankful for what we have. But you'd always rather spend Thanksgiving at home." Brandon Spincer, who was spending his first Thanksgiving away from his children, replied sarcastically, "Yeah. In all honesty, I'm kind of tired of being around Antonio Mason."

Earlier that day, Spincer had been asked what, aside from his family, he was most thankful for. His answer: "I know a lot of guys say things just because it sounds good, but being a senior, I'm really, really thankful that we were able to play the season even though it didn't turn out the way we expected. I'm thankful that I got to go out and play football this year, because we could have easily gone the other way."

Despite the feelings of thankfulness floating around the room, many players couldn't help missing the family they'd hoped to see on Thanksgiving. Jordan Ellis, for instance, had never missed a Thanksgiving with his family. Back home, Ellis' mom, Kim, enforced the rule that everyone must help out with the meal. So while neighborhood kids had played football in the street or watched a game on TV, Ellis had spent his time in the kitchen with his mom. His yearly responsibilities included marinating and meat tenderizing. This year, his family was gathering in Jackson, Mississippi, and because of the extended football schedule, he wouldn't be there. "I guess my little brother will have to step up," he said, referring to his yearly tenderizing duties. "Big shoes to fill."

Bubba Terranova could sympathize with Ellis' sadness. While other players lightheartedly swapped stories and barbs, Terranova sat solemnly by himself, poking at his sweet potatoes. Beckman, his close friend, was still recovering from the shooting. His mother was in another city. He knew how despondent she was; they'd spoken on the phone earlier in the day. And the football season, the one thing lifting her through the Katrina aftermath, was almost over.

Their last game would take the team back to where their journey had begun: Jackson, Mississippi. The plan was to stay in Jackson on Friday night and drive 90 miles on Saturday to Hattiesburg, where Southern Mississippi's Golden Eagles were waiting for them.

That Friday in Jackson, Terranova was sitting in his hotel room when he heard a clamor in the hallway. He heard someone yell, "Beckman's here!" Terranova hopped out of his room, followed the buzzing, and spotted his dear friend, who looked pale and thin. It had been only 12 days since the accident, but Beckman wanted to see his teammates before the final game. Terranova approached him and carefully put his arms around him, and they hugged just as their parents had at their last game. Ninety days after their first stay in Jackson, the team was reunited there once again, only this time, it was the end of the season, and the players couldn't even begin to list how everything had changed.

On Saturday, November 26, Tulane arrived in Hattiesburg for a game they were supposed to have played in early

September. The season opener, postponed because of the storm, was now the season finale. These conference rivals had played annually since 1979, but Tulane had won just seven times. Some of those Tulane victories have become classic moments in the team's history: the inaugural matchup, which Tulane won 20-19; Tulane's 1993 17-15 win in Hattiesburg, which snapped a six-game losing streak; the 2002 upset that came in Tulane's Hawaii Bowl season. This season, Southern Miss had a lot on the line; they had to beat Tulane, or else they wouldn't be bowl-eligible.

The game day conditions were miserable. The sky was as gray as cigarette ash, and dark clouds hovered overhead. Rain fell continuously all afternoon, varying only in its intensity. Patti Terranova looked at the sky and wondered how else could the season be ruined. The Tulane cheerleaders on the field, lacking the appropriate rain gear, wore their winter coats, so each of them was a different color spot on the sideline. All season, they'd driven or flown to the games. Having been displaced to other schools for the semester, they would spend days planning and nights driving, just to attend a football game and lead the cheers of a sparse crowd during a loss. But they felt that Tulane, now more than ever, needed all the support it could get. They didn't want the players to feel that the student body had forgotten them. "Our hearts were there," cheerleader Erin Healan said. "So we had to be there, too."

Pride had carried the players through much of the season, especially after they were branded bowl-ineligible. They'd felt it at several key moments throughout the season, and they felt it again that day in the game against Southern Miss. Early on, Tulane made its presence felt: Spincer had sprinted across the field toward a running back and forced him out of bounds;

Lucas had crunched a receiver on a screen pass, and moments later, he leapt into the air to disrupt a receiver, causing an incomplete on third down. With absolutely everything to play for, the Southern Miss offense could not get into a rhythm on its first two possessions. But neither could Tulane's offense. The Elliot experiment, where Scelfo had tried out the red-shirted freshman as starting quarterback, was almost over; he floundered in his two drives, and Scelfo pulled him and put Ricard in to play the next two possessions. Elliott subbed in for another possession, but sprained his ankle, ending his season perhaps just minutes before it would have ended anyway. The quarterback job for the rest of the afternoon belonged to Ricard, who almost immediately tossed an interception.

Tulane's defense continued to stymie Southern Miss' big plays, but allowed quite a few little ones, letting the opposition score a touchdown and notch two field goals. Midway through the second quarter, the home team had 13 and the visitors were scoreless. But something was happening in the trenches. For the first time since the game against Southern Methodist, Tulane's offensive line was consistently creating holes. The passing game may have been in shambles—it was the reason why Tulane didn't score in the first half—but the running game was working better than it had in a long time.

Running back Matt Forté had tallied 87 yards in that SMU game, but hadn't matched that total all season. By the season finale, he wasn't even ranked among the conference top-10 in any rushing categories. Forté, like so many of his teammates, had failed to live up to any of the preseason hype. In his case, before the season began, the coaches compared him to Mewelde Moore, the former Tulane running back who then played in the NFL. After Forté's success during the 2004 season, he and

Ricard had been expected to be a one-two punch the following year. But by November of 2005, neither of them was even starting.

Against the Golden Eagles, however, Forté had run for 77 yards in the first half alone, finishing with 137 on a season-high 27 carries. He ran for a first down nine times. Overall, the Tulane offensive line, with seniors McGee and twins Matt and Joe Traina, played one of its better games.

The weather gods, though, were on no one's side. As the game progressed, conditions on the field became so unbearable that the cheerleaders were forced to head for the stands and cheer with the fans as opposed to in front of them. The rain fell in sheets across the grass. Patti Terranova squinted through the rain, trying to find her son, who was on the sideline after missing a pass intended for him earlier in the game. He suffered from severe pain in his knees, a condition caused in part by his having to walk up and down the eight flights of stairs in the Ruston dorm several times a day. He had played through the pain in previous games, but it had intensified that final week, and so he told coaches that during this last game, he could only play sparingly. He'd made a catch early in the game, a 2-yard screen pass, and he made the tackle after Ricard's first interception. And so, in the last game of his college career, Bubba Terranova had as many tackles as receptions.

The Golden Eagles made another field goal right before halftime. Down 16-0, Tulane couldn't nab a first down on its first three plays of the second half. Coach Scelfo decided to shake up the game; he drew up a backup-punter-to-linebacker pass. Barrett Pepper, still replacing Beckman, awaited the snap. And Cannon, the linebacker, darted vertically up field and corralled the pass, a 28-yard completion.

On the very next play, Forté ran right and put on the brakes, while tight end Bobby Hoover swallowed the closest defender. Forté then sliced between a pair of defenders, and while they pounced onto the wet turf, he rumbled for a couple first downs. When he finally went out of bounds, a 26-yard total gain, Tulane had the ball on the Golden Eagles' 22. It was Tulane's best field position all day. From the 15 on third-and-4, Forté ran for 3. They settled for a field-goal attempt, but Jacob Hartgroves missed the kick, and Tulane remained behind 16-0, with 7:53 left in the third.

To make matters worse, Shawn Nelson, Southern Miss' brawny tight end, caught a pass toward the middle of the field on a third-and-5 once they regained possession. The Tulane cornerback Youmans had two hands on Nelson's back, but Nelson shook him off and sprinted 50 yards toward the end zone, leaving Tulane's players in the dust. When Nelson crossed the goal line, Youmans had barely reached the 10. The score was now 23-0 with 4:47 left in the third quarter. Youmans dropped his head, knowing the game was very likely over.

Tulane did score on the ensuing possession on a Damarcus Davis catch. During the drive, Ricard had thrown a beautiful 32-yard pass to Preston Brown. But after the Green Wave defense forced a punt on the next drive, Ricard eventually threw his second interception of the day. Southern Miss, smelling a bowl bid, notched another field goal to take a 26-7 lead, which would soon be the final score.

On the final play of Tulane's season, a Southern Miss fullback escaped from the lunging arms of two Tulane defenders. The safety Boger rammed his body into the fullback's stomach, but Boger bounced off of him. Finally, defensive end Frank Morton jumped on the fullback's back, smothering him after a

9-yard gain. The clock ticked off its last few seconds, and the game—and Tulane's season—was over.

The home crowd erupted; their team was bowl-eligible. Mothers shrieked. Players from both teams merged on the field, shaking hands and slapping backs. Southern Miss player Luke Johnson grabbed the public-address microphone at midfield and proposed to his girlfriend. Joe Traina, the senior Tulane center, walked by some fellow offensive linemen. He spotted his mother, Lorraine, in the first rows of the crowd. In a similar display of affection, she yelled, "Hey baby, I love you."

Cannon, his jersey smeared with mud and grass, walked toward the locker room with his helmet in his left hand and his head down. He finished the game with a team-high 11 tackles, finishing with 114 for the season and 437 for his career. Only three players in Tulane history ever accumulated more.

Outside the locker room, Preston Brown spoke about the same things he'd mentioned that day at the Dallas Doubletree, when the team was in the midst of falling apart. He talked about how thankful he was to be a part of the team, regardless of their record. In the same season that he made his first collegiate catch, Brown led Tulane with 47 catches and six touchdowns, earning Third-Team All-Conference honors.

Inside the locker room, Chris Scelfo stood proudly in front of his team, his green long-sleeved shirt drenched with rain and sweat. "This is an experience," he said in his hoarse voice, "that no one can take away from you." He told his players he loved them, and that he loved what they had accomplished. After the postgame speech, the seniors presented Scelfo with a plaque. His eyes were so wet with tears that he couldn't read the inscription.

Thanksgiving

Each player left that locker room carrying Scelfo's speech, and the memories of the entire season, in his heart. Standing near the team busses were dozens of mothers and fathers, siblings, classmates, and coaches' wives, all ready to congratulate the Green Wave on completing the season. Hidden among the masses was Patti Terranova, still wearing the jersey Bubba had given her years ago. Bubba emerged from the locker room, sifted through the crowd, and found her. He enfolded her into his arms, hugging her tight against the rain, against the inevitable end of the season that had sustained them both.

CHAPTER 19

Endings

$\mathcal{F}$or Bubba Terranova, dressing up usually meant tucking in his shirt. But just weeks after their final game, he found himself in Orlando, Florida, wearing a tuxedo. He was there, along with Scelfo, to represent Tulane at a December college football awards dinner. The Green Wave had won two prestigious awards that honored their season of perseverance: the Football Writers of America Association's Courage Award and the Disney Spirit Award. For Terranova and his teammates back in Louisiana, these awards validated their season, regardless of their record. The awards proved that people knew their story and had been inspired by their determination to play despite adversity, and that they were right to be proud of what they'd accomplished.

After the awards ceremony, Chris Scelfo mingled with his colleagues, including Mack Brown of Texas and Charlie Weis of Notre Dame. Joe Paterno, the legendary coach at Penn State, shook Scelfo's hand and said, "Tough year, Coach." Kevin White, the athletic director of Notre Dame, made a point to find Scelfo; White had been the athletic director at Tulane from 1992 to 1996. White proudly shook Scelfo's hand and said, "I don't understand how you did it."

Early on in Tulane's season, after the close loss to Mississippi State and the following week's domination of Southern Methodist, the players had become momentarily wide-eyed; maybe, they thought, they could still make a bowl game. Isn't that the plot of every sports film, every Disney movie about a struggling team? Against all odds, Tulane would muster the energy to win it all—after some close calls, of course—because that's the storybook ending they deserved. But as this plot became more and more unrealistic as the losses mounted, the players remembered what Scelfo had first said in the Dallas Doubletree: This season would not be measured in wins and losses. Sure enough, eight losses later, Disney honored the team's extraordinary decision to stick together and play with its Spirit Award. Scelfo had been right; the award had nothing to do with winning games. But in the minds of those watching, Tulane had a winning record; they'd beaten adversity.

The ceremony was a glorious moment for Tulane football, one that Terranova clung to days later as he slept on his mother's couch. Tulane's campus, where he planned to live the next semester, would not reopen for the spring semester for another month. His home in Slidell was gone, and so was his car. Bubba and Patti had moved in with Patti's father and stepmother in a New Orleans suburb called Harahan, generally untouched by Katrina. What remained of Bubba's belongings sat stored in the garage. Football and its structure were behind him, and all he could see in the future was cold, biting uncertainty. Without football to distract him, the reality of the rebuilding work ahead of him and his mother settled in, and with Patti at work during the days, he felt lonely and frustrated. "He was like a prisoner," Patti said.

During the days, Patti taught junior high across the Mississippi River in an area called Avondale. Although it had been a long time since she'd lived with her father, he still saw her as his little girl. Things were a little strained, with three generations cramped inside the same house. Patti's father often cooked dinner at 5 p.m., which was early for Bubba and Patti, so they were often not home, and Patti's father would begin to worry that something had happened to them. Patti often felt guilty for receiving her father's help—he was paying most of the family's bills—as well as the help of various government agencies. She thought about all the people who'd lost everything, including their jobs, and wondered whether she should accept the government help that others might need more than her. At least she still had a job, and that was more than a lot of New Orleans residents had.

For Patti, Tulane football had been the equalizer. Sunday through Friday were difficult to get through all fall. Saturday was the goal; Saturday was therapy. The day after Bubba and the team walked off the rain-soaked field at Southern Miss, Saturday became just like Monday or Thursday. There was no refuge.

In the months following the 2005 football season, the city of New Orleans was full of both hope and hopelessness. Coach Scelfo sensed this paradox every morning as he drove into the city for work, slithering through the patched-up West Bank, then across the Mississippi River, past the unopened Wal-Mart where looters reigned during Katrina, past the abandoned homes in the lower part of Uptown, and finally onto the campus of Tulane, where some buildings where bustling with students, and other structures, such as the football practice facility, were barren.

From Katrina's first raindrops, Tulane President Scott Cowen had shown his commitment to reopening the Tulane campus. He spent the initial days after the storm breaking into buildings to search for food, hot-wiring a golf cart to use as transportation, and sleeping in the gym. Once the levees broke and the campus was flooded, he used a motorboat to navigate across campus. Eventually he found a dump truck and used it to get to safety, driving it through the deep water to Audubon Park, where he was rescued by helicopter.

Tulane University was a stalwart presence in the community and, as football coaches proudly told the parents of recruits, was also one of the nation's more prestigious schools. *U.S. News and World Report* consistently ranked Tulane in the top 50 national research universities. But the hurricane and the subsequent flooding had reduced this bastion of education into a swamp. The Uptown Campus was inundated by floodwater, which crept into nearly every building, causing a reported $200 million in damages. With students spending the fall semester at nearly 600 different American universities, the school suffered a reported $100 million in operating losses. Tulane had 6,000 employees, making it the largest employer in Orleans Parish. Only a couple hundred of these employees, most of them part-time workers, lost their jobs after the storm; the others had been paid throughout the displaced fall semester.

President Cowen knew that getting his university back on track would take extreme measures, and that all the while, he had to maintain the university's dignified and dynamic reputation. Belfor, a company that specializes in damage restoration, was hired to clean the campus, and Cowen announced that the second semester would resume, as usual, on January 17.

However, Tulane had to make numerous controversial cuts to ensure the viability of the overall university. Tulane's Board unanimously approved Cowen's plan to eliminate Newcomb College, which was the nation's oldest degree-granting college for women. Cowen merged Newcomb with Tulane College, its liberal arts counterpart for men. And Tulane also dropped all but two of its engineering majors, citing a dwindling number of students in that major. The reasoning made sense, but not to the engineering students, many of whom now aspired to help rebuild the levees in post-Katrina New Orleans. Both these decisions were met with protests and petitions.

Cowen, a sports enthusiast, also made the difficult decision to suspend eight of the lower-revenue athletic teams: men's and women's tennis, men's and women's golf, women's soccer, women's swimming and diving, men's track and field, and men's cross country. The suspension would save the university millions, but that didn't make it any easier for Athletic Director Rick Dickson to give the 98 athletes affected by it the news, especially considering that sitting among that group was his son, Doug, who ran cross country for the Green Wave.

Despite the cuts across the board, when the school reopened its doors on January 17, a reported 87 percent of the fall semester students returned to Tulane's campus. That included the entire Green Wave football team. In a sport where transfers are common and occur annually, not one offensive or defensive starter transferred from Scelfo's team, nor did any key reserves from the 2005 team. Many experts had assumed that several of the players would transfer after the disappointing 2005 season; back in November in Ruston, Izzy Route, perhaps Tulane's best junior defensive player, said transferring was something he was definitely considering. But come January, he was on Tulane's campus, flashing his wide smile. Moreover, not one of the 12 assistant coaches left. Players and coaches alike returned to campus buzzing with enthusiasm even though they accepted the reality that Tulane and its football program were still works in progress.

The biggest challenge ahead of them was recruiting a solid incoming class. Tulane's extensive recruiting files and films were left behind in New Orleans when the team first evacuated. They didn't even have access to their files until October, a good month into the high school season, prime time for recruiting. Assistant coaches rarely got the chance to visit high schools and see games, as they were using any time off to visit and repair their homes. Other coaches realized the incredible disadvantages Tulane faced in this area of college football. Southern Methodist coach Phil Bennett even gave Tulane his list of recruits, an extremely gracious gesture from a rival coach.

When they did recruit, the sales pitch was a little tough. They had to sell a losing football team that currently had no campus; a home stadium, the Superdome, that had sustained millions of dollars in damages; a university that wouldn't begin operating until two weeks before signing day; a city that was being pieced together by ineffective government agencies, while half the population already there had decided not to return to the very place the coaches were trying to sell. Tulane coaches could only imagine what opposing recruiters were whispering in recruits' ears about their program. But Tulane's biggest recruiting foe was CNN. Every night, the network swamped the airwaves with images of a ravaged New Orleans. These pictures went a long way toward convincing potential recruits that Tulane was not the place for them to begin their college football careers.

What's worse, these recruits could not make official campus visits during the season because, of course, there wasn't an operating campus, so they never got a taste of what the Tulane really had to offer. In normal seasons, Tulane would welcome dozens of fresh-faced high school students during home game weekends, where the students would get a taste of college life and some Louisiana cooking. Recruits would then spend Saturday afternoon on the sideline at the almighty Superdome, watching Tulane play on the same turf the Saints would the next afternoon. The only official visits for the 2005 season occurred in two hectic weekends in January of 2006. Scelfo made it mandatory that parents accompany their kids on the trip, to see the city and campus with their own skeptical eyes. Many prospects declined to come. Thirty-four did, which was about 14 fewer than previous seasons.

They came with questions: Where will I live? Are other students coming back? Is it safe? One mother was so concerned about safety, that Coach Scelfo offered her a bulletproof vest and around-the-clock security if she would come. Her son ended up signing. So did 23 other recruits, making up a recruiting class with which Scelfo was actually quite pleased.

A big snag was Kevin Moore, a quarterback from Flower Mound, Texas, who committed in April of 2005. He kept his promise to Scelfo, and hoped to become the next great quarterback at Tulane, following Shaun King, Patrick Ramsey, J.P. Losman, and the incumbent, Lester Ricard. "Tulane is going to bounce back," Moore told the *Times-Picayune* on signing day, "and I want to be part of helping them." Another recruit, defensive back Chinoso Echebelem, had people in his ear all winter, telling him negative things about Tulane. But he wore a Tulane hat on signing day, and said that the perseverance of the 2005 team had inspired him, so he wanted to be part of the 2006 team.

But for all the excitement about returning to school and the buzz surrounding the new recruiting class, there was still this sobering reality: The school's football facilities remained in disarray. For months, the pent-up frustration in Ruston was countered with the hope of a refurbished New Orleans. But when the football team returned to campus in January, the athletic hub was inoperable. The Wilson Center, once the sparkling headquarters of Tulane athletics, was barren and coated with dust. Five feet of water had stormed through, ruining millions of dollars in equipment and washing away generations of memorabilia. In one hallway, a bulletin board still stood, congratulating Tulane's reigning conference champions in men's tennis, women's tennis, women's golf, and women's swimming and diving—all teams that had been suspended.

The football locker room had been gutted, as had the weight room. That winter, Director of Football Operations Dennis Polian wandered through the empty Wilson Center, sighed, and said, "We need 'Extreme Makeover: Athletic Department.'" Outside, Tulane's two practice football fields were inoperable, the synthetic turf waiting to be replaced.

Thanks to the efforts of Dickson and proud alums, the Wilson Center reopened on March 30, and one of the two practice fields was ready for spring ball on April 3. Most universities were nearing the end of spring ball when Tulane began. And then, because not every academic major had summer courses available, only a small percentage of the team could stay on campus for summer school. In previous years, the majority of the team would be in New Orleans, taking classes, working out, and hanging out as a team. But that bonding time would not be something that year's team would have.

"It was a continuation of the previous year," Coach Scelfo said of the setbacks. "Just a different address." Still, during spring practice, when players were on the field, there was a sense of purpose. Practice was separate from everything else that had made their return to New Orleans difficult. Chachere, the linebackers coach, had had a phone glued to his ear over the past few months, talking to everyone from his wife, who was in Virginia because their Louisiana home had been destroyed, to a high school coach with an attractive recruit on his roster, to FEMA representatives. But on the practice field, Chachere could lose himself in the intricacies of the game he coached. The phone stayed in the office. "Football," he said, "kept me sane."

And as the spring progressed, as seniors graduated and recruits came to campus, as things began looking like they used to, football took up more and more of the time that Katrina's aftermath had once demanded. For everyone involved, it was a welcomed, long-anticipated change.

CHAPTER 20

New Beginnings

$\mathcal{A}$t the end of the spring semester, before the 2,200 Tulane graduates could throw their caps in the air, before comedienne Ellen DeGeneres arrived on stage in a bathrobe, saying, "I was told everyone would be wearing robes," former president Bill Clinton spoke to them about the year they'd been through.

"Dream your dreams," he said, "and try to live them. For life's largest disappointments are not rooted in failures or mistakes. Anybody who's lived long enough has made a fair share of both. The greatest disappointments are in the absence of passionate commitment and effort—the sense of not having tried. You may not end up exactly where you want to go in life, but following your stars will guarantee you a marvelous journey. And it will enable you to begin again."

"Begin again" was just what the Green Wave planned to do. Spring ball had gone well; summer had passed by quickly. Soon enough, the football team found itself a year removed from the day they'd evacuated. On August 29, 2006, a new season of Tulane football came out onto their practice field. The sun blazed overheard. A sweaty ESPN camera crew lingered on the sideline hoping to catch a sound bite that would somehow encompass the gamut of emotions on the field. Sportswriters conducted one-year-later interviews with Scelfo, this time nowhere near the Dallas Doubletree. Coach Scelfo wore a tucked-in, white-collared shirt, green shorts, and a white ball cap with the Tulane logo. After practice, he would make numerous television appearances, live from New Orleans, to discuss the anniversary.

Voices carried across the field. Eric Schumann, the defensive coordinator, walked around the field with an awkward, hasty gait, and then, when he saw something he didn't draw in the play book, his displeasure leapt out of his mouth and into the ears of his defense. Offensive line coach Don Mahoney yelled instructions in a gruff, almost indecipherable bark. Garret Chachere, with a fresh crop of linebackers, bellowed at his players, his voice full of a deep, passionate resonance. Added into these sounds were the hard pounding of pads, many high-pitched whistles, and the grunts of college football players ready to begin again. It was a symphony.

On the adjacent field, the kickers and punters practiced. Chris Beckman, now a senior punter, was there after having made a full recovery from the hunting accident; he'd undergone two life-saving surgeries before making it back to the field. There were many new faces on the field, too. These belonged to the freshmen that had decided to sign with Tulane even though the school had gone 2-9 and its campus had been in shambles just months earlier. They'd chosen to be a part of this rebuilding process on and off the field.

Although these freshmen were now part of the Tulane family, it was still strange to see them wearing numbers that had belonged to the recently graduated veterans. Alex Wacha wore Sean Lucas' No. 31. Some of the returning players switched their numbers altogether: tight end Gabe Ratcliff switched to No. 5, which had been worn by Spincer; receiver Damarcus Davis now wore Cannon's No. 11; senior linebacker Terrence Peterson, who had seldom played in the past, switched to Terranova's No. 17 for his final season. It was as if the returning players subconsciously didn't want those numbers given to a newcomer, a freshman who might not truly appreciate what—and who—the number represented.

Ricard was on the field that day, too. He'd kept his original number. He had the appearance of a self-assured signal-caller, though the biting reality of the 2005 season was ever present. He felt that he was a better player than what his statistics during the hurricane year suggested. Ricard, with every pass at practice, felt like he had to make up for lost time and that he had to show everyone that he could reach his predicted potential. Moreover, Scott Elliott, the backup quarterback who had taken snaps in Ricard's place several times during the 2005 season, was hanging around. Ricard remembered the pain of standing impotently on the sideline. On one hand, he felt like he was the undisputed leader of this team, the one guy who had the ability to rejuvenate the Tulane offense. On the other hand, he was vulnerable, a senior quarterback surrounded by question marks, with an antsy backup and an antsy coaching staff. Ricard, like the rest of the Tulane staff, was more than ready to begin again.

Jordan Ellis, now the starting middle linebacker because Anthony Cannon graduated, showed up to the August 29, 2006 practice with long, wavy, untamed blonde hair. His shaggy locks were soon drenched with sweat, as was his green jersey. He wore gray gloves, white pants already streaked with grass stains, tall black socks, and white shoes. Although taking over for the impressive Cannon would be a tough job, Ellis had an air about him. He carried himself with a cool confidence— something the previous season's trials had given him.

Ellis had spent the summer of 2006 cleaning up his hometown of Pass Christian, Mississippi, about 70 miles west of New Orleans. He'd also spent as much time as he could with a fishing pole in his hand. "You can get out there," he said, "and it's like nothing ever happened." What remained of his parents' house were only the 10-foot wooden beams, as stripped and naked as the gigantic tree in their frontyard. They'd never found their roof. "The best way to picture it," Ellis said, "is like a big hand grabbed it and just ripped it off." The entire town had suffered substantial damage at Katrina's hand, having been inundated with an estimated 35-foot storm surge.

The Biloxi Sun Herald, the biggest newspaper in the area, had published a long feature about him that summer. The story said that Ellis would be Tulane's starting middle linebacker. Everyone in town, it seemed, had read it. Strangers would come up to Ellis and ask him, "How's football?" or say, "I can't wait to come watch you play." Ellis felt the additional pressure, but he saw it as motivation, because he knew his hometown would be watching him.

That day, just as he had in the Dallas Doubletree a year earlier, Ellis soaked up Scelfo and Chachere's every word. He peppered his coaches with questions. Ellis admittedly felt pressure as the sudden starter, but he was excited to be learning on the job. He worked hard on the field if only to forget where he'd been emotionally just a year earlier.

During practice, Scelfo walked slowly from position to position, listening to his assistants relay the messages that Scelfo had relayed to them earlier in the day. Then, for minutes at a time, he would stand like a general and watch his team run plays. He was grappling with questions that bounced around his head, and there were plenty this season because of the loss of so many key players, notably Spincer, Cannon, Lucas, Terranova, and essentially the entire offensive line. Those players had all moved on.

After becoming the first person in his family to graduate from college, Brandon Spincer had skipped out on the commencement ceremony to instead attend rookie camp for the New Orleans Saints. It was a magical experience for him because he'd grown up worshiping the Saints. For a few days, he was one of them, but the dream soon died. He was cut after the rookie camp.

Although disappointed, Spincer had already planned his next move in case football didn't work out for him. He wanted to work to help the children of the New Orleans community, having been inspired by kids like Cordell, the boy he'd taken under his wing while living in the Ruston dorm. Spincer remembered all those kids in his neighborhood who looked just like him and talked just like him. He remembered how vulnerable they all were to negative influences, and he decided to dedicate himself to helping them. Spincer began working for Girls and Boys Town, a national organization that served at-risk, abused, abandoned, and neglected children across the country. Spincer said of the work, "I enjoy waking up every morning knowing that my presence at a place can have a positive impact on a child who is going down the wrong path."

Spincer also planned to dedicate his time to rebuilding New Orleans. He was becoming increasingly concerned with the city's rising crime rate and the way people seemed to turn to violence more readily than they used to. "I'm scared for my kids," Spincer said. "The violence and the negative things that are going on, it can only get worse. I live here, and I see that it's not getting better. I worry about my kids. I'm going to try to expose them to positive things, but at the same time, they have to live in this city."

Bubba Terranova was no longer a Tulane player, either, but he was still a Tulane student. Many of his 2002 freshmen class-mates had graduated from Tulane that past spring, but while living in Ruston after Hurricane Katrina, Terranova had found classes irrelevant and unimportant in the face of everything else going on. His attitude resulted in two Fs. His mother cried when she heard about his grades, but Terranova looked on the bright side; he was still a senior, living in on-campus housing and rooming with Beckman in a dorm just a couple football fields away from the rec center.

Just like when her son was a college freshman, Patti Terranova still drove to her son's dorm in Uptown to retrieve his laundry, except now, she drove back to her father's home to do the wash. She hadn't been to her home in Slidell in nearly a year, but that area of town was slowly picking itself up. Patti and Bubba still talked on the phone every single day, sometimes multiples times, even if it was just to see what the other was doing. Of the continued laundry service, Patti said, "It's not as if he can't do laundry. I just want to see him as often as possible."

Up in Detroit, a world away from the August 2006 practice in New Orleans, Anthony Cannon was surviving the Lions' cuts and getting closer to becoming an NFL rookie. A month before training camp, the Lions signed Cannon, a seventh-round draft pick, to a three-year contract. Cannon had been a starter at Tulane since arriving on campus. For the first time in nearly a decade, however, it was likely that he wouldn't be starting, which was a weird feeling for him. Still, Cannon had packed his swagger and brought it north with him. Even though he understood he would play on special teams that season, he still believed in his athleticism and that he would eventually be important to the defense.

Back on Tulane's campus, football practice ended. Coach Scelfo called his team to the center of the field. Every player took his helmet off and got on one knee. It had been an average practice; the team had been inconsistent for much of the preseason, trying to get reacquainted with each other while working in 13 new starters. Coach Scelfo stared at his team. In his Louisiana drawl, Scelfo reminded them that only one year earlier, they'd been on the floor of the Jackson State gym, unsure as to whether or not there would even be an upcoming season. Now they had the luxury of playing on a brand-new practice field in the comfort of campus. His message was simple: Appreciate where you are, and show that appreciation with every move you make in practice and on the field.

He also reminded them that their opponents had circled Tulane on their calendars, marking them as easy to beat. If Tulane was 2-9 last season, how much better could they be the following year? Scelfo reminded them that they were, in fact, a good team. But they had to believe it—and show it in practice. By circling the games on their calendars, other teams were disrespecting Tulane. The Green Wave needed to take that personally, and practice that much harder to prove to opponents that they shouldn't have taken Tulane lightly.

Scelfo then revealed the election results for team captain. Receiving 90 percent of the votes was Preston Brown, the senior receiver from Camden, New Jersey. After having inspired his teammates with his 2005 speech at the Dallas Doubletree, Brown had emerged as Tulane's most consistent offensive player that season. His efforts were now being rewarded. He stood up, walked toward Scelfo, and shook his mentor's hand while the other players applauded.

In addition to Brown's new beginning as team captain, he had also recently begun a different journey: one as a new father. Asked if he was scared about being a dad, Brown said, "No, there aren't too many in things in life I'm scared of." It was an attitude his team would take on as well as they embarked on the 2006 season.

Epilogue

$\mathcal{F}$rom the beginning of the 2006 season, players and coaches alike recognized the difficult road ahead. Tulane was down for 12 games that
season, as opposed to the usual 11, so there would
be no bye week. The Green Wave would start the
season with three road games, two of them against
teams from the mighty Southeastern Conference. In
fact, they would play three teams from that conference in 2006, all on the road: Mississippi State,
Louisiana State, and Auburn. The latter two were
both in the top 10. Those games were nothing more
than paydays; the big schools invited Tulane to play
there and paid them six figures to do so. The big
schools had the money to spare, could make it back
in ticket sales, and would gladly splurge for what
they assumed would be an easy win. And Tulane
needed the money after the hurricane had largely
wiped out the athletic program. Tulane had originally scheduled a game against a Division II team to

nab an easy win, but that game was dropped and the Auburn game took its place on Tulane's schedule, something Scelfo learned about while reading the morning newspaper rather than first hand from his boss, athletic director Rick Dickson.

Scelfo knew that the public perception was that his team had no reason—no excuse—to not be successful. He also knew he would have to wring out all the success he could from this team just to win six games for bowl eligibility. He felt that if they didn't win six games—which would not be easy, considering they'd lost so many starters—he might be in some trouble.

Their first game was against Houston. Though many things had changed, Patti Terranova was still in the stands to support her team. When she spotted No. 17 on the field—Bubba's old number, now being worn by Terrence Peterson—she began to cry.

The home team won the coin toss, and before Patti's face could dry, Houston was in the red zone, moving 70 yards downfield to score the first touchdown. Although players Izzy Route, Lester Ricard, and Matt Forté made effective plays during the game, Tulane was still making mistakes, including fumbling a kickoff. Houston won the game 45-7. Perhaps more impressive than the score itself was the fact that Houston had accumulated 621 offensive yards—an astounding total.

Three days after the Houston debacle, Scelfo, who rarely attended the offensive line's positional meetings, charged into the room where his assistant, Don Mahoney, was conducting just such a meeting. He gave them a simple message: You've got the skill, but you don't have the focus. If Tulane had any hopes of having a successful offense, these boys had to realize their importance and focus on their jobs.

The next game was a rematch against Mississippi State. The Bulldogs had defeated Tulane in the 2005 season opener in

Shreveport. The night before the game, Preston Brown and some of the other seniors called a players-only meeting where they motivated the team by talking about family and about strength in numbers. The pep talk must have been effective; Tulane had a 14-7 lead at halftime and went on to win, their first victory on the road against an SEC team since 1989. This was also Tulane's first win since the Southeastern Louisiana game back in 2005, nine losses ago, when they hosted the Division II opponent in Baton Rouge's Tiger Stadium.

After the victory against Mississippi State, Tulane returned to Tiger Stadium, this time as an opponent of the nationally ranked LSU Tigers. Tulane didn't have a chance against this SEC team, one of the best defenses not only in the country, but also in LSU history. They lost 49-7.

The Green Wave, now 1-2, returned to New Orleans for something foreign and surreal: a home game. The refurbished Superdome stood proud and robust in the New Orleans skyline. After $185 million in renovations and repairs, the Superdome, like the city, was open for business. On September 30, 2006, Tulane played its first game in the Superdome in 665 days.

Game day felt awkward. Tulane had become so accustomed to uncomfortable situations that waking up in New Orleans and driving just a few minutes to a game actually felt abnormal. But they soon remembered what it felt like to be home when they walked into the Superdome and saw the vibrant green "T" on the 50-yard line and the thick green "TULANE" in each end zone. For the first time in a long time, the stadium was full of Tulane fans—people who had had to follow the 2005 season via Internet. Brandon Spincer was there, as were Bubba and Patti Terranova. For the first time in three decades, Tulane had assembled a marching band of 45 honored Tulane students who wore gleaming uniforms and performed "Do You Know What It Means to Miss New Orleans."

Scelfo decided to jolt the offense into action, calling for a fake punt pass early in the game from Tulane's own 6-yard line—a huge gamble, but Scelfo felt that he and his staff had broken down the film so well during their preparations for the game that the move was almost a sure thing. Beckman received the snap in the end zone and spotted Michael Batiste wide open, but the pass went incomplete. It took SMU just three plays to score a touchdown. By the fourth quarter, Tulane trailed 20-7, but Ricard suddenly completed several passes, including two for touchdowns. With 7:52 left, Tulane led 21-20. That lead lasted only a few seconds; SMU's Jessie Henderson ran 102 yards to score on the punt return. After a Ricard fumble and another SMU score, Tulane's first game back in the Superdome ended like most of those games on the road—in a loss.

Tulane got its first home win that season against Rice the following week. Next they faced Texas-El Paso, a team that had defeated them in the Ruston game in 2005. Preston Brown caught 11 passes, nearly doubling his season total, but it would not be enough to give Tulane the victory. The Green Wave was now 2-4 heading into the game against Auburn.

The Green Wave played hard against the statistically impressive Auburn team. Brown caught nine passes for 139 yards and seemed unstoppable until an Auburn tackle twisted his ankle. That day, Tulane accumulated 389 offensive yards against Auburn, something even LSU or Florida hadn't done. The Green Wave entered the red zone four times, but had mustered only two field goals. In the end, Auburn won 38-13 in a game that should have been closer.

Brown didn't play the next week in the game against Army because of his ankle, which had swelled every afternoon in practice. Forté again emerged as an offensive leader, running for 124 yards and two touchdowns. Tulane won the Army game 42-28, giving them a 3-5 record.

As Tulane prepared for the next week's game against Marshall, Brown continued to subject his ankle to the rigorous practices. "You could tell he was in pain," running back Ray Boudreaux said. "And he didn't care." Brown planned to play that Saturday.

The Marshall game started ugly, with the opposition leading 21-0 by the end of the first half. But in the second quarter, on a key third down, Tulane receiver Chris Dunn caught a 22-yard pass for a first down, and that drive ended with a Tulane touchdown when Ricard completed a pass to the still-injured Brown. Forté scored the game's next two touchdowns, making the score 21-21. Late in the third quarter, Forté was tackled and suffered a severe ankle injury. He was out for the game, and for the season. Tulane had scored 21 unanswered points, but after Forté's injury, Marshall came back to do the same thing, winning the game.

With their record at 3-6, Tulane's last hope for maintaining bowl eligibility was to win against rival Southern Miss. But the team proved to be unfit for the challenge. By the game's fourth quarter, Tulane's offense had managed only 74 yards total. Ricard hadn't completed a pass in the game's first three series, and his replacement, Scott Elliott, had only managed to make six first downs in three quarters. Scelfo put Ricard back in late in the fourth quarter, the team down 24-3. At one point on first down, Tulane received three penalties—two false starts and a delay of game—before even snapping the ball. On first-and-25, after a gain of just 2 yards followed by another incomplete pass, Chris Scelfo made an unprecedented move. He called for a punt on third down, hoping that his players would learn a lesson from that kind of embarrassment and that it would make them perform better in games to come. He wanted to send the message that the way they were playing was completely unacceptable. But the message was lost: "They should have been insulted, they should have been embarrassed," Scelfo said, "but they weren't any more insulted or embarrassed than I was."

The loss made Tulane bowl-ineligible, but the next week, they nabbed a win in a close game against Central Florida. The win was the 37th of Coach Scelfo's career, making him the second-winningest coach in Tulane's 112-year history.

Tulane had one game left to play in the season, a finale at Tulsa that upcoming weekend. But tragic news hit the team early that week and inarguably destroyed their focus. Their former teammate, Brandon Spincer, had been murdered.

On November 20, a Monday night, Spincer had dropped off his girlfriend at her home in the West Bank of New Orleans. Her ex-boyfriend ambushed him and shot him in the street.

The Jefferson Parish morgue had contacted Chris Scelfo; they'd been told that Spincer played football for Tulane, and they needed someone to identify the body. Scelfo accepted the responsibility, recognizing how hard it would be for Brandon's parents to see their son in a body bag.

On the drive back home after recognizing the body on the gurney as Brandon's, Scelfo felt the way he had when he'd lost his parents, yet also like a father. Spincer's story was supposed to have a fairytale ending. He'd overcome adversity so many times—remaining focused on his future despite being surrounded by crime and despair in his youth, working hard to make it back on the field after becoming academically ineligible, playing through the 2005 season despite being separated from his children—that it was hard to accept the true conclusion. It was not the way Brandon's story was supposed to end.

On Tuesday, the day after Spincer was murdered, the players united in the locker room to dress for practice, the atmosphere marked by silence and sadness. Out on the field, Scelfo spoke to the grieving team. "Guys, we've been through a lot together," he said. "We'll never understand why something like this had to happen. But you all know Brandon as well as I do, and he would not want us to feel sorry for ourselves, or for him. He's in a better place, we all know that." Despite their heavy hearts, each member of the team knew they had a game to play—their final game of 2006. On that day, they would each wear No. 5 decals on their helmets in honor of Spincer. Gabe Ratcliff, who had switched to No. 5 for the 2006 season, would wear No. 2 against Tulsa.

Later that afternoon, Spincer's parents, Barbara and Barry, met Scelfo in his office. Barry cried throughout the entire meeting. Scelfo gave the parents photographs of Spincer during his playing days. He tried to tell them how much Spincer had meant to him, though he found it hard to express his feelings with words. He also promised the family that he would take care of the funeral, assuring them that Spincer would be laid to rest with dignity. Scelfo then called a few close friends, including New Orleans Saints running back Deuce McAllister. They raised enough money for the funeral, and it was set for the following Monday.

Tulsa was 7-3 and on their way to a bowl game. With the events of the previous week all too fresh in their minds, Tulane lost their final game 38-3, finishing the season 4-8. Scelfo knew that his job would go under review in the coming weeks, but his focus wasn't on himself; his focus was on the Spincer family, the Tulane football family, and the upcoming funeral.

Services for Brandon Spincer were held on November 27 at the Watson Memorial Teaching Ministries in Uptown New Orleans. Inside the chapel, sunlight refracted through the green stained-glass windows onto the congregation. Many of those touched by Spincer were in attendance. Coach Scelfo, in a black suit and tie, fidgeted in the pew next to his wife, visibly uncomfortable. Next to them sat numerous Tulane assistant coaches, some wearing sunglasses to hide their tears. Spincer's children, seven-year-old Branisha and two-year-old Brandon Jr., sat in the second row with their mother.

The 2006 team arrived in their green jerseys, which they'd tucked into their dress pants. After the final game, Preston Brown had thought he would never put on his Tulane jersey again. But he put it on one last time to honor his friend. Brown looked down at the program that had been passed out to the congregation. The mother of Spincer's children had written a paragraph for it, and part of it read, "Now I'm left here to do this alone." Brown's own daughter was not yet one year old, and the words only deepened his grief.

At the front of the room lay Brandon, dressed in a suit, in an open casket. In the quiet of the room, Brandon Jr. spotted his father in the casket. Oblivious to the meaning of the situation around him, Brandon Jr. smiled and said in his high-pitched voice, "There's my daddy!"

A woman introduced Coach Scelfo of Tulane University to the congregation. With a slight hunch in his back, Scelfo slowly walked up five stairs to the pulpit. He had not planned on speaking at the funeral, but that morning, Spincer's parents had asked him to do so. He had nothing prepared. He looked out at the packed congregation, at his wife, at his players, at his fellow coaches, at the Spincer family, at Brandon right below him.

"Branisha, you don't know this," he began, "but the reason everyone in this room got to be close with Brandon was because of you. He wanted to stay home for college and be with you, and later on, with Brandon Jr. And that's really one thing I wanted to talk to everyone here about who knew Brandon. I had the good fortune to know him. He lived his life the way he wanted to live it. He was very accountable. And if you spent any time with his parents, you know where he got it from. He was responsible for his own actions. He made a difference. A lot of times, we talk about people who hope they made a difference. Brandon Spincer, bless his heart, made a difference. Each and every one of you in here, in some form or fashion, was affected by him as a leader. He was a leader for all of us. He was someone who will be sorely missed. But there's one thing I can tell all of you in his family, one thing I know Brandon wanted more than anything; he wanted you all to be there with him. And the way you're going to do that is follow in his footsteps. He lives through Jesus Christ and he chose the right things in life. As someone who thought the world of him and thought of him as a son, I'll tell you this; we'll all see him again, if we're on that path."

An organ began to play a melodic and soulful hymn. Everyone was invited to walk in a line to the front of the sanctuary to offer their condolences to Spincer family and touch Brandon one last time. After the procession, Pastor Tom Watson took the stage.

"How do we make sense out of nonsense?" Watson asked in his slow voice. "It's one of the most critical times in human history, particularly in the city of New Orleans and the region of the south, with all we've had to endure. We have tried to make sense out of all we are doing, and here we have a family that lost a young child. I'm sure Barry and Barbara Spincer are trying to make sense out of all of the nonsense, and I believe all of you in the audience are trying to do the same thing. How do you have a young man like this, on his way, doing the right thing, going to the right school, making the right choices, and all of a sudden, a senseless act takes his life?

"In order to make sense out of nonsense, we must have courage. For a black man to graduate from Tulane, that took courage. Somebody say 'courage.'" Scattered about the congregation, people yelled: "Courage!"

"The sad fact is," the pastor continued, "we have more black men in prison than in college, so it was courageous for Brandon to come from the background he came out of, to face Tulane University, and not only go there, but go there and do well. Somebody say 'courage.'" The pastor's passionate voice ascended and reverberated through the congregation. Occasionally, a woman would stand up. Some folks helped him finish his sentence. When the pastor asked everyone to lift their hands to God, Brown not only lifted his hands, but wiggled his fingers.

"God is still in control, " the pastor said. "Shout it out and let every one in New Orleans know!" The congregation responded, "God is still in control!" The pastor shouted and proceeded to paraphrase Psalm chapter 119, versus 54-56. Then he began brimming with fervor: "God is trying to tell us Brandon did not die in vain. Can I get a witness here?"

After every sentence, the organist slammed the keys. "Yes, it was way too early! But read the obituary! He made it at St.

Augustine! He made it at Tulane University! He made it at Girls and Boys Town! He made it uptown! He made it downtown! The obituary tells us he made it to the House of the Lord!" The audience feverishly clapped, and the services drew to a close.

One day after the funeral, Coach Scelfo had to fly to Tampa, Florida for a recruiting trip. While there, his cell phone rang. It was Rick Dickson, Tulane's athletic director. Scelfo's heart began to race. Scelfo hastily flew back to New Orleans, and the two met, man to man, just as they had in September of 2005, when Scelfo told his boss he was going to Ruston either as a father or as Tulane's head football coach. Scelfo's genuine passion had saved him that day, but there were too many opposing factors this time around.

Dickson informed Scelfo that he was no longer Tulane's head football coach.

"The direction of the football program is not satisfactory," Dickson told the New Orleans media later. "We must do better. We must be competitive in our conference. We must be eligible for postseason opportunities on a regular basis." The 2005 season was supposed to be Scelfo's pinnacle year, but Hurricane Katrina had altered that destiny. In Dickson's eyes, the fact was, hurricane or not, 2005 was just one in a streak of four consecutive losing seasons. Some of the boosters were getting restless. And the fan base, flimsy even before the storm, needed a jolt.

Going into the 2006 season, Scelfo knew that six wins would preserve his job, and anything else would make for a debate about his future. But at the end of the day, he felt like he deserved one more year. He felt that the 2006 season was an extension of the hurricane season, and his team, even though they were home in New Orleans, was still on an unequal playing field with their opponents. Building a football team is a year-round task. Yet from

December of 2005 until April of 2006, there was little cohesiveness with Tulane's team while they waited for the practice facility and weight rooms to be rebuilt. In the summer, the team had been scattered all over the country because summer school had been hard to coordinate after the storm. Throw in the challenges of the LSU and Auburn games, two paydays that could have been replaced by winnable opponents, and four wins might have turned to six right there. Then there was Forté's injury in the Marshall loss when the game was still tied at 21, and he proceeded to miss Tulane's final three games. A difference in any one of these factors could have changed the season's record, but those in charge saw only the numbers 4-8.

Scelfo's team had done everything that was asked of them from the moment Katrina showed up on the radar. They had proudly emblemized Tulane athletics' mantra during 2005: "To carry the torch, be the face, and represent the name of Tulane." Said one of Scelfo's friends upon his firing: "We got burned by the same torch they told us to carry."

○ ○ ○

In the coming months, Scelfo embraced his free time by attending his son's baseball games, helping his daughter with homework, and actually getting home in time for home-cooked meals with Nancy. He could finally take a deep breath and reflect on everything he and his team had been through.

Two decades ago, he had signed up to be a coach, one of many ambitious 20-somethings who wanted to shape lives and build a program. By 2007, Chris Scelfo had redefined the word "coach." After one of the worst natural disasters in American history, which ravaged the homes of the majority of his football team, Scelfo injected his players with purpose and perspective—his recipe for perseverance. His players learned what it meant to be a teammate when there wasn't fame or glory to fall back on, when being a teammate meant being a brother. He had helped a family through an accidental shooting, and another family through a murder, all while being a rock for his football family, as well as his two kids at home.

During the hurricane season, Scelfo taught his players to harness their emotions, to play for others, to seize the day and not let the day seize them. Along the way, his team lost a whole bunch of games. But he felt like he was a winner, especially when he thought of all the success members of his team had found once that season was behind them. Anthony Cannon was preparing for his second season as a Detroit Lion, where he embraced special teams duties with the same zeal that had made him a Tulane star. Lester Ricard went undrafted, but was invited to the Jacksonville Jaguars rookie camp, where the talented quarterback tried to harness the confidence that, at times, made him look like the NFL quarterback he always thought he should be. Assistant coach Garret Chachere took a job with the University of Memphis, Tulane's conference rival. Chris Beckman, the country boy punter, found himself in the most unlikely of places: Winnipeg, where he latched on to a Canadian football team. Bubba Terranova became a Tulane graduate. He remained in New Orleans, where his mother, Patti, continued working as a schoolteacher.

Preston Brown, the proud 2006 team captain, graduated from Tulane in May 2007, his girlfriend, Tiana Cornish, and their daughter, Ayanna, watching him from the audience. He had learned perseverance from Chris Scelfo, and then taught it thoroughly to his teammates for two seasons. He said of the experience: "Losing sucks, definitely. But in my mind, we're always going to be champions for just enduring that season. Forget the record . . ."

Scelfo understands exactly what Brown meant. With everything behind him, the coach now knows for certain that he and his players are, and always will be, winners.

Acknowledgments

First we must thank Jim Amoss, Doug Tatum, and Kevin Spain of *The Times-Picayune* for allowing this book to be written. Also, we'd like to thank Doug Hoepker, Jennine Crucet, and everyone at Sports Publishing for allowing this book to be published. Thank you to both Tulane University and Louisiana Tech University, two proud schools that became symbols of perseverance during the months after Hurricane Katrina. James Davison was an essential reason the team could stay together in Ruston, and for that we are grateful to him. Also, thanks go to Joe Bullard, who helped us out with transportation while we were in Ruston.

Families were an important part of this project, so we'd like to thank the authors' own supportive families, the families of Tulane football players, and the Tulane football family itself. We'd like to especially thank the Beckmans and the Terranovas for opening up their homes and their hearts for this project, and the Spincers—we wrote about Brandon with our hearts, and he remains to us an inspiration.

Of course, every member of the 2005 Tulane football team was integral to the writing of this book. Thank you to everyone, notably those who shared his or her time: Chris Beckman, Ryan Bewley, Tra Boger, Ray Boudreaux, Preston Brown, Anthony Cannon, Garret Chachere, Chris Dawson, Jordan Ellis, Erin Healan, Bobby Hoover, Sean Lucas, Don Mahoney, Antonio Mason, Chris McGee, John Mendow, Michael Parenton, Lester Ricard, Israel Route, Michael Sager, Darren Sapp, John Sudsbury, Bubba Terranova, and Matt Traina.

Thank you to Deuce McAllister of the Saints for his heartfelt foreword. It meant so much to us that you wanted to be a part of this project.

Also, thanks to Lance Barrow at CBS Sports, John Underwood and Donnie Duncan of the Big 12, and the late James Wilson Jr., for their support.

Finally, thank you to the city of Ruston for opening your arms to us. And thank you to the city of New Orleans for giving us a reason to coach, a reason to write, and a reason to persevere.

—Chris Scelfo and Benjamin Hochman

ABOUT THE AUTHORS

CHRIS SCELFO served as the head football coach at Tulane University from 1998 to 2006. He coached the Green Wave to victories in two bowl games and developed current NFL stars Patrick Ramsey and J.P. Losman. The New Iberia, Louisiana, native and Louisiana-Monroe graduate lives near Athens, Georgia.

Benjamin Hochman is a journalist working for the *Times-Picayune* in New Orleans. He spent the 2005 season with the Tulane football team, capturing and documenting the Green Wave players and coaches. Hochman won first place for sports feature writing in 2005 and 2006 from the Louisiana-Mississippi Associated Press Managing Editors, the Louisiana Sports Writers' Association, and the New Orleans Press Club. A graduate of the Missouri School of Journalism, Hochman lives in New Orleans.